NATURALLY
PSYCHIC

NATURALLY PSYCHIC

Awaken Your Intuitive Abilities

Karen Harrison

WEISER
BOOKS

This edition first published in 2025 by Weiser Books, and imprint of
Red Wheel/Weiser, LLC
With offices at:
65 Parker Street, Suite 7
Newburyport, MA 01950
www.redwheelweiser.com

ISBN: 978-1-57863-879-6

Library of Congress Cataloging-in-Publication Data

Names: Harrison, Karen (Charboneau-Harrison), author.
Title: Naturally psychic : awaken your intuitive abilities / Karen Harrison.
Other titles: Everyday psychic : a practical guide to activating your psychic gifts
Description: Newburyport, MA : Weiser Books, 2024. | Includes bibliographical references
    and index. | Summary: "Discover how psychic you really are with this comprehensive and
    practical guide to developing and honing your psychic skills. This book shows you how to
    awaken your natural psychic abilities and experiment with psychic tools to get answers,
    guide your decisions, and enrich your life"-- Provided by publisher.
Identifiers: LCCN 2024057660 | ISBN 9781578638796 (trade paperback) | ISBN
    9781633413719 (ebook)
Subjects: LCSH: Parapsychology. | Psychic ability.
Classification: LCC BF1031 .H265 2024 | DDC 130--dc23/eng/20241223
LC record available at https://lccn.loc.gov/2024057660

Cover and interior design by Brittany Craig
Cover and interior images by Muse Artist/Creative Market,
    MaxCompose/Creative Market, Creative Market/Isabelle Salem, iStock
Typeset in Adobe Garamond Pro

Printed in the United States of America
LBM

10 9 8 7 6 5 4 3 2 1

To Diane, Ysleta, Del, Morgan, and Sophia,
the wise and wyrrd women of my family,
for your support, teachings, and
fascinating philosophical discussions.

ACKNOWLEDGMENTS

I would like to thank my husband, Jeff, for his thoughtful reading of passages of this book. Whenever I was struggling to explain something with clarity, his words and ideas were the perfect nudge.

I am blessed with many friends and colleagues who work with dedication and wisdom in the world of spiritual and psychic development. Thanks to all of you for the amazing work that you do!

CONTENTS

INTRODUCTION

I was fortunate to have been born into a family interested in the many alternative ways of looking at the world and interacting with it. My grandmother, Ysleta, and her sister, Del, were interested in psychic phenomena, dream interpretation, séances, hauntings, telepathy, spiritualism, psychic animal communication, and much more. My grandmother gave me my first deck of tarot cards, my great-aunt took me to my first séance, and my mother took me to my first past-life regression. These women all considered the non-physical world to be just as real as the physical one, and agreed that there are many different and valid ways to get information in addition to the basic five physical senses. They were happy to share their ideas and experiences with me from an early age.

Growing up in this rich environment, I was taught to listen to my intuition, to delve into the wisdom of my dream-life, and to use any psychic tool in which I had interest. I was taught to not fear the disembodied, and to interact with them to obtain knowledge and give comfort. I came to understand many valuable things, such as how normal it is to be psychic and the importance of using your more subtle senses in addition to your physical way of interacting with the world. I learned that, really, while you can use tools like tarot as a springboard to help you interpret the ways that energy patterns are setting up and moving, the knowledge always resides *within you*. Psychic tools are just that—tools—and it is your mind, your emotions, your sensitivity, and your awareness of what your intuition and psychic senses are bringing to you that are the true basis of psychic work. It's your job to learn how to access the knowledge in healthy, clear, and balanced ways as you discover which psychic tools work the best for you. You may find that the innate psychic talents that reside within your intuitive sensitivities are the best tools for you, and that you prefer not to bother with physical implements such as tarot cards. Or you may find that jump-starting your psychic sessions using something like the tarot or I Ching serves as a helpful springboard for your intuition, moving you quickly to the heart of the question that is being examined. It's up to you.

I've heard many times over the years, from people who are not familiar with such things, that being psychic or consulting a psychic is something to be feared. Some people believe that just because a psychic states that an event will likely happen, or because you have a vision that makes you uncomfortable, that the statement made by the psychic or the vision that you have had is predestined and will always come true. This is not the case at all and not because the psychic is a fraud or because your vision was wrong. The event is not predestined to take place precisely because you have become aware of its potential in your future. The awareness of this potential allows you to be proactive—to change the patterns in your behavior or in your attitudes, in your emotions or in your thoughts, thus allowing you to act and think differently. In this way you can consciously and purposefully move your future in another direction and away from an outcome you do not want. By using your psychic senses to become aware of the potential future that you are creating, you can deliberately act upon that knowledge and guide your own destiny.

If the likely outcome that is sensed psychically could not be altered or diverted, I don't think there would be much use in knowing about it. Listening to your psychic side, deciding how you feel about that outcome, and then acting in response to the information presented allows you to make informed decisions and choices about how to change the things in your life and environment that are creating that likely future. It's like traveling to any destination. As you travel, you are on a road that has many different routes that you can journey on to reach your intended destination. All roads contain many turn-offs or paths that you can take instead—you can even stop or back up. You can continue driving straight ahead into the lake which you have glimpsed before you, or you can turn onto a side street and go another way to your desired destination. Acting upon the psychic information that you have received works the same way. When you see what lies ahead, you can change your actions, your thoughts, your reactions, your feelings, or your approach to the situation, and thereby change the outcome, thus altering your future.

As you uncover, exercise, and hone your talents, you will sometimes find that the information you receive is not what you were hoping to find—the outcome looks like something you would prefer to avoid, or that will not work out the way you wanted. When reading the future, do not despair if you see something that you don't like. The future is not a cut-and-dried affair. When reading the future, you are seeing what is most likely to happen if you or your querent (the person for whom you are reading) proceeds on the same path which is now being traveled. People can change their perspective and reaction to foreseen events, and by those changes, alter the outcome of events and therefore the future. If you psychically encounter a possible future that you don't like, analyze the components that are creating that outcome, and then meditate on how you can change those components into circumstances which will benefit you. Examine your current approach and analyze what you need to change about yourself, both internally in terms of your emotions and perceptions, and externally in your actions and words. Those insights could help lead to the result you're looking for. Then your next question using your psychic abilities should be: "What do I need to do to achieve what I want in this situation?"

This is the value of divination—discovering the underlying issues from the past and present that are acting to create the future. If you know the most likely outcome from the actions you are now taking, you then have the knowledge you need to make the future your own. By your new actions, you now have the ability to alter your own future. Your destiny is not set in stone. By getting a reading and hearing the answers you (or the psychic who is reading for you) do not make the future happen. A psychic reading is literally a reading of the energies working within a situation. By changing your approach, you change the outcome. That is the value in getting a reading. If something was bound to happen no matter what you did, why would you want the reading? A reading empowers you to make decisions, direct your life, and open to the changes that will improve and enrich yourself.

What is being psychic? According to *Merriam Webster's Collegiate Dictionary*, 10th edition, psychic is 1: of or relating to the psyche, soul; 2: lying outside the sphere of physical science or knowledge; 3: sensitive to nonphysical or supernatural forces and influences; marked by extraordinary or mysterious sensitivity, perception or understanding. I would say that I mostly agree with those definitions, with a few exceptions.

In response to definition number 1: being psychic is definitely related to the psyche (the inner self, the soul, the subconscious mind) because that is precisely where a person becomes aware of, and receives, nonphysical information or experiences. This information or experience must then be brought forward into the conscious mind and interpreted. It is the recognition and reception of subtle information by the psychic senses, coupled with the interpretation by the conscious mind, that gives us the information that we are seeking. When we utilize our psychic talents to examine a question, we also are analyzing our options and our choices in regard to that question. This receiving of subtle information via the psychic energies (which are present everywhere and all of the time) coupled with the rational, linear, conscious mind analysis of this information, allows us to make informed choices and decisions regarding any changes we deem appropriate and beneficial in order to create the future that we desire.

In response to definition number 2: while currently, psychic experiences may lie outside the sphere of observable physical science, I doubt that it will be too much longer before we understand in more linear, conscious terms how and why psychic experiences and events happen and what they might mean. Scientists are experimenting with many types of energy expressions and modalities to discover why and how they work. For example, within our medical sciences, it has become accepted and almost commonplace for nurses to utilize the energy healing method of Reiki in their day-to-day interactions with their patients. Using Reiki, the healer will manipulate a patient's energy field to help the patient to relax, to find the best place to insert a needle for a blood sample, and to aid in the body's healing process. They have found that Reiki training enhances their ability to "know" or "sense" things and be more aware of the many subtle signs that their patients are giving them. I am confident that as more studies on the use of energy healing modalities and medical care occur, we will begin to comprehend the how and why of these energy methods and their effects on the human body.

In response to definition number 3: this is where I will quibble. Being psychic certainly involves being sensitive to nonphysical forces—that's the point, isn't it? However, these are not supernatural forces; they are completely natural, physical forces that are just not as easily perceived or experienced by the basic five senses that most of us possess, due to the subtle nature of these forces or energy patterns. Your everyday senses encompass much more than just your simple five physical senses—taste, touch, smell, sight, and sound. Would you deny that you have a sense of smell simply because you can't see the smell, hear the smell, or touch the smell? Being able to use and rely on the psychic senses is not extraordinary, it is something we are all born with. And being able to use and rely on your psychic senses is not mysterious—it is something that you can develop and use in a conscious, purposeful manner to aid in every aspect of your life.

Think about the things you have already experienced that involved one or more of your psychic senses. Every moment of your life, since the time you were an infant, you have used your more sensitive (although outwardly unacknowledged by most of the world) senses as you assessed situations and determined how you wanted to react to them. How did you know that that innocuous-looking person at the bus stop was potentially dangerous? They may have appeared perfectly normal and calm at initial sight. But you might have unconsciously noted a certain look in their eye, or felt a butterfly sensation in your stomach as you approached them. This unconscious (psychic) response alerted you to the fact that you needed to keep a closer eye on them, or even keep on walking to stay away from the energy that they were transmitting and the potential danger they might exhibit.

Why did you instinctually pause at the green light, even though your eyes did not at first detect the car hurtling around the corner to run the red light? Because you *sensed* a quickly shifting energy pattern and were fast enough to react to it on an unconscious (psychic) level. Your eyes could not detect the accelerating car because it was out of your line of sight around the corner, but your psychic senses were on alert and aware on your behalf, transmitting the unconscious information to your brain that you should not move forward.

We have all felt a slight prickling sensation at the back of our heads and turned around to see someone staring at us. We felt the energy of their focus on us and this subtle feeling prickled our conscious awareness and senses. These are all natural yet unconscious assessments of energy patterns that we encounter every day as we go about our mundane business. The trick is to use your more sensitive senses in a conscious way, acknowledging them and acting on them when they occur so that you can strengthen these senses by their use. In that way you can employ all of your senses, physical and subtle, to know what is going on around you at all times. Yes, some people are born with more active psychic gifts, just as some of us can sit down and play a piano without a lot of instruction. But with use, practice, and conscious, deliberate exercising of our natural intuition and inborn psychic tools, all of us can utilize our psychic talents and abilities to enhance our lives. Being psychic is not extraordinary or mysterious—it is a natural state of being for everyone.

So what are psychic readings, and how do they work? First, let's define the term "reading." A reading is when a psychic sets out to literally "read" the energy of a situation and all the permutations surrounding it. These components can include the attitudes of the people involved in or affected by the outcome. The emotions that the situation stirs, as well as the past and present actions of the people involved, all have a bearing on how the situation moves forward and is likely to turn out. Reading is an assessment of all of the energies surrounding the question that is being asked, followed by a conscious analysis of how those energies will tend to affect the future. Does there seem to be resistance, blocks, or challenges to the outcome that is being worked toward? Does the energy flow around the question feel smooth, easy, and straightforward? After receiving and analyzing the information given by a reading, you are empowered to make changes, choices, and adaptations to the situation in a conscious, thought-out manner which will create your future.

A psychic may choose to use a tool like tarot cards, or looking at the aura of a client to get answers. They may decide to toss the runes or meditate to connect with their guides. Perhaps they prefer to consult their dreams for information, or gaze at the symbols offered by the residual tea leaves in the bottom of a cup. They may pick up and handle an object to sense the energies present within it. The method used will be the choice of the psychic reader, based on their preference and what type of tool they have determined works best for them, or for the type of question being examined. There are all kinds of different ways to obtain psychic information, and all kinds of tools that can be utilized. It is really up to the psychic and what he or she has discovered through their own practice that determines the method they choose to employ. They will use the tools that seem to work best for them as an individual.

Different psychic readers have varying ideas about where their talent comes from. Many psychics feel that their psychic power is inherent within themselves. They believe that when they read they are tapping into the present energy flows of an individual, and the psychic tool they use (tarot, pendulum, channeling, etc.) is simply a medium to help trigger their intuitive ability. Others may speak of tapping into a "universal mind" or "universal consciousness" to get information about a situation, group, or individual. Either way, when a psychic performs a reading, they are accessing a feeling and a flow of energy connected to a situation, and the likely outcome of that situation, to get the information they are seeking.

As the psychic works, they are tuning all of their concentration and focus into the subtleties of the situation, and analyzing and interpreting the energy from thoughts, emotions, actions, and attitudes that surround the situation. You may choose not to use physical psychic tools like tarot or runes in your work; instead, you may simply link up with the energy flavors present directly through your own senses and abilities. As you work to hone your talents, you may find that the way you obtain information is that you have a clairsentient experience as you "feel" the energy—you literally have some physical sensations that experience has taught you mean specific things. You may "see" the outcome clairvoyantly as you receive visions, colors, and images that you interpret. Or you may receive a "knowing"—an experience of claircognizance. In this type of psychic information gathering, after tapping into the energy around the question, you receive information about how the energies are coalescing and "know" where that energy flow is taking the situation. You may experience clairaudience, wherein you "hear" the answer. You may feel like you are listening to information that is being dictated to you either within your mind or even slightly outside of yourself, within your aura, as you interpret and convey that information to your client.

Regardless of how you psychically receive your information, the fact of the matter is that you are in charge of your life and your destiny. The information and the outcomes to the situation that are received through your subtle senses reflect the thoughts, actions, and emotions that are present and active in the question being asked during the reading. By changing some or all of those reactions, the querent—whether it is you asking questions for yourself or for an individual you are counseling—can change their own future and therefore the outcome to the question. That is the value of receiving a reading—the discovery of whether or not the actions that are taking place now will result in the outcome desired. If a person's actions will bring the result they are seeking, the answer to the question will be to continue on the current path. The information received will often address specifically what actions are being taken now that are bringing success to the outcome, so that the querent can concentrate on doing more of the same. But if what is being brought to the situation is actually working against the success of the endeavor, the reading will tell specifically what actions are being taken that are getting in the way, and give ideas and options for changes that can help turn the outcome into what is desired.

This book shows you the myriad ways that you can access your inner voice—your intuition and natural psychic abilities. You'll play with some psychic techniques and work on communicating with your inner psychic voice using the innate tools you came equipped with in your body and your psyche when you were born. You will also explore methods that will help you to determine the accuracy of the information you are receiving, tune into the centeredness of your inner self, and learn how to turn off distractions that can cause you to misunderstand the psychic "hits" you are getting.

While you will be exploring various techniques and methods of obtaining information psychically, the emphasis in this book is on readily accessible psychic tools that strengthen your basic inborn talents. These tools will allow you to access your subconscious mind, use and strengthen your intuition, and then consciously analyze the received information. Your analysis will happen as you work at interpreting the meaning of your emotional response to the information received. Your intuitive interpretation of that emotional response and other information you receive via visions, knowing, psychic seeing, or clairaudience will be due to your developed sensitivity to the energy currents surrounding you and whomever you choose to counsel.

Using the exercises outlined in this book, you will be concentrating on psychic tools that are receptive and subjective in nature, like psychometry, dream work, interpreting the aura, and working with guides. There is a structure and foundation to subjective psychic work with these kinds of subjective intuitive tools, but without the memorization inherent to other psychic methodologies like tarot and rune reading, which employ intuitive abilities but also require memorization of their symbols and pictures in order to fully understand the information you are getting. With this book, you will hone your talents in psychic development and master techniques that will make your readings more accurate. You'll examine psychic opening preparations and methods to help you read for yourself and for others with accuracy and confidence.

Each chapter in this book specifically addresses a different method of obtaining information psychically. Each psychic modality is defined and explained, and exercises are provided to give you a chance to experiment and play with each type. The chapters are ordered to enable you to use this book as a workbook if you like— each subject and its exercises serve as another piece that can help you to master the next psychic modality addressed in the next chapter. But each chapter is also complete unto itself. If you are the type of person who prefers to skip around a bit, and you want to engage in simply those psychic subjects that hold your current interest, all the information and ways to work on and with that psychic method are here, ready for you to play with.

And, although this book is written to inspire the beginner and enable them to expand their worldview and psychic talents, it is intended for the experienced psychic as well. You all have particular psychic tools and talents that you turn to regularly—it is my hope and intention that experienced psychics who read this work will also enjoy learning what may be some new viewpoints, as well as new skills, that you can add to your repertoire.

I have read professionally and taught classes in psychic development and the use of the various tools of the psychic since I was a teenager. There is not a day that goes by that I don't find help and enjoyment while using the natural psychic talents that I was born with. Whether it is interpreting a dream from the night before that has information for me, meditating on a past-life experience that gives me a tool to use today, or handling an object that tells me its story from its residual energy patterns, something occurs each day that gives me insight and new clarity. I am excited to share with you my experience from that professional perspective to help you expand your world and your talents.

CHAPTER 1

Sensing, Understanding, and Using the Flow of Energy in Psychic Work

Energy and its flow is being unconsciously experienced by everyone, all of the time. We are all surrounded and impacted by the action and movement of energy twenty-four hours a day. When you feel the warmth of the sun on your skin, you are feeling the electromagnetic energy of the sun, which is expressed in the energies of heat and light. When you get a sudden chill and perhaps the hair raises a bit on your arms upon entering a room, you are experiencing the residual electromagnetic energy of an event that occurred there, or of a person who was once in that place. The energy frequency residue has been left behind in that room, just like when you get a whiff of perfume that has been left behind by someone who was once there. When you feel a slight tingle on the back of your neck and then turn to observe someone looking at you, you are experiencing the outflowing electromagnetic energy from that individual as they focus their attention on you. When you feel a small, subtle tug at your diaphragm, you are sensing the electromagnetic energy pull of a person or entity seeking to connect with, and perhaps partake of, your own energy flow. What you are sensing or feeling in each case is the electromagnetic currents, wavelengths, and frequencies produced by the outflowing radiation of electromagnetic energy inherent in each experience.

You are familiar with many physical forms of electromagnetic energy waves and how they work in your daily life. You experience these energy frequencies and their results when you turn on your radio and receive the audible sound waves of the news or music. When you turn on your television or computer monitor, you see images and hear sound. When you answer your phone, you are responding to a call that is composed of electromagnetic energy waves, which have been transmitted by a satellite through space, or by electrical impulses that come to you by way of electrical transformers to the receiver of your phone. When you speak to the person standing next to you, they are receiving your transmitted vocalized sound wave frequencies through their own receivers—their ears and their brain. You can't see any of these electromagnetic frequency waves with your physical eyes, but you do experience their results through your physical senses.

What is this electromagnetic energy, and how does it work? Electromagnetism manifests and acts as both an electric field and magnetic field. These fields are simply different aspects of electro-magnetism. Basically, two sides of the same coin, if you will. A changing (transforming) electric field generates a magnetic field; while a changing (transforming) magnetic field generates an electric field. This effect is called electromagnetic induction, discovered by scientist Michael Faraday in the 1830s (Williams, L. P. *Michael Faraday, A Biography*. New York, NY: Basic Books, 1965).

When energy is being released or sent out, it is acting as an electrical impulse in a series of pulsating frequency waves. The reception of this electrical impulse is transmuted into magnetic force by the act of receiving it.

The human brain is both a transmitter (electric) and a receiver (magnetic). On average, each person's brain contains about ten billion nerve cells, called neurons. Each of these neurons is connected to other neurons throughout the human system by the conductor of electrical impulses within the body's system—the synapse. A synapse is the junction at which a nerve cell (neuron) communicates and transmits information to another cell. An example of this electrical neuron communication is when you make a decision to move your foot. You decide, consciously or unconsciously, to move your foot, and the electrical impulse in your brain's neuron instantaneously communicates, using the synapse, to the nerve cells in the muscles of your foot, causing it to move. Your brain and your response can work the other way, too. Perhaps your foot steps on a sharp rock. Immediately the nerve cells in the foot communicate to the neurons in your brain that you are sensing pain and you have an instantaneous reaction of "ouch" and you remove your foot from the source of pain.

Thoughts, perceptions, and memories are created and contained within the brain, an organ made up of physical, organic mass. The brain uses the electrical currents and magnetic impulses within its mass as its method of retrieving or processing knowledge, experiencing and interpreting the world, and making decisions regarding how to react to inner and outer stimuli. These thoughts, perceptions, reactions, and memories each generate electrical currents within the brain, and are part of what creates and makes up our own personal magnetic energy field. Our feelings and emotions contribute electrical energy, too, as our bodies respond to emotional stimuli, such as joy or fear.

It is by the nature of these electromagnetic energy flows within the brain, and the energy fields of people, animals, and objects that the many techniques of acquiring psychic knowledge occur. We know that, like everything in the universe, our earth has its own electric current and its own magnetic field. For example, subtle energy paths on and beneath the earth's surface, called ley lines, are discernable using dowsing rods or the psychic senses, due to strong electromagnetic transmissions. These energy lines typically lead to, and connect, power centers such as Stonehenge and Avebury in England, or indicate energy vortexes such as those located in Sedona, Arizona. In Chinese practice, these ley lines are called Dragon Lines or Dragon Currents, and form the basis of the practice of feng shui. In dowsing, it is the magnetic quality of water which allows the dowser, using his or her own subtle energy sense or dowsing rods as a tool, to locate aquifers of water, springs, and streams.

Many creatures, such as homing pigeons, salmon, turtles, and bees, navigate using their inborn sensitivity to the earth's magnetic field. Studies performed in the late 1980s and early 1990s showed that each of these types of animals possess a small amount of a magnetic substance called magnetite within their tissues, leading researchers to conclude that the magnetite within their systems sensitizes the animals to the magnetic field of the earth and the specific magnetic frequency of the geographical location that is imprinted within their particular DNA memory (Kirschvink, J.L., A. Kobayashi-Kirschivink, B.J. Woodford [1992] "Magnetite biomineralization in the human brain." Proceeding of the National Academy of Sciences, USA). Thus, without a map or a GPS, these animals instinctively find their way back home or to their spawning ground through their sensitivity to, and unconscious awareness of, the magnetic frequencies in the earth. Magnetite has also been discovered in the human brain near the brain's magnetically sensitive pineal gland, a gland that secretes hormones that affect the entire body, including melatonin, which regulates our sleeping cycles. It is the pineal gland that has always been associated with human psychic abilities and the Third Eye.

This is how we receive psychic information. Everything in our universe emits an electromagnetic force. Everything in our universe has a magnetic field—in humans this magnetic field is often called the aura or auric field. People have magnetic fields, places have magnetic fields, and trees, animals, and stones have magnetic fields—all created by the radiation of their own electromagnetic energy. In humans and animals, it is primarily thought processes and emotional responses that create, inform, and make up this energy flow. By tuning in to the electromagnetic currents of an individual and their thoughts or feelings surrounding a question or concern, information that is clear and helpful can be obtained by a variety of psychic means. For example, when working with clairvoyance or techniques of psychometry to ascertain the energy flow and flavor of an object, such as a ring or letter, the psychic is tuning in to the residual energy that is attached to the object as well as the person for whom they are consulting.

Of course, psychic information can sometimes be clearer or more easily interpreted when a direct question is asked, but we also receive psychic information unconsciously and randomly all the time as we encounter people who are emitting waves of information by way of their thoughts, focused attention, or elevated emotions. We pick up these bits of information unconsciously through our psychic senses. Places and things that we encounter can also send us an energy "impression" through the residual energy patterns present in their auric fields, due to circumstances or events that involved the place or thing in the past. We are constantly bombarded by electromagnetic energy waves as those frequencies pass through our own energy fields and even through our bodies: interacting with another person's energy field, using a cell phone, working on a computer, watching television, experiencing the magnetic energy field of the earth, sensing the gamma rays produced by lightning, and feeling the electromagnetic waves emitted by the sun. You might think that this cacophony of energy would drive us mad, but we are beings of energy ourselves, and we are equipped to filter out what we don't need, absorb what we do need, and pay attention to the parts that we want.

It is our conscious awareness, and understanding of, the electromagnetic action of energies in the body, the mind, the emotions, and the general environment that is vital to the clear use of psychic abilities. When we choose to deliberately engage our psychic senses and subconscious minds in the receiving, examination, and analysis of the information contained within these energy flows, we acquire psychic data, knowledge, and clues. We then use the information we have acquired through our subtle senses to analyze and diagnose what is happening within a person, as well as the events and circumstances which are surrounding that individual. This leads us to informed conclusions about how that individual is acting within their personal world, as well as the world as a whole, thus navigating and creating their own future. By initially accessing the information via the psyche's sensitivities to energy flows and flavors, the subconscious mind begins to work with the knowledge it accesses—deciphering the symbols, feelings, colors, and facts that are being presented in a psychic reading. The subconscious mind then partners with the conscious mind to translate that information into knowledge and advice that can be verbalized, verified, and shared. The person for whom we perform the reading then has the information that they need in order to make decisions and determine what actions they need and wish to take in regards to the situation.

This work is not limited to the reading of the subtle energies of a person. Sensing and recognizing the type of energy flows within a space can also be part of a psychic's work, if they are seeking to understand what types of events may have happened in a home, building, room, field, or any other physical location. Energy residue can be left in a place due to ongoing emotional distress experienced in that place. This residual force can also be due to a haunting or an act of violence that has occurred within the space. Once the energy flow information residing in a location is received and analyzed, the psychic will then understand what type of techniques or tools will work the most efficiently to clear or transform the energy in a home, a public building, or other space if that is the goal.

Energy residue is not created or left in a space by only negative events or emotions—it can also be created by positive actions, thoughts, and feelings. There is nothing so peaceful as walking into a church and allowing the calm and solace that resides within that structure from the energies of the prayers and healings that have occurred there to soothe and quiet the soul.

When reading for an individual, receiving, diagnosing, and understanding the different types and flavors of the energies working within that person gives the psychic insight into the individual's day-to-day life, their motivations, challenges, fears, strengths, emotions, and attitudes. Accessing the energy "flavors" of an individual—their thoughts and feelings, potential health issues—and the energy currents presently acting upon a person by a coworker, spouse, or family member, allows the psychic to feel and receive information from those energy flow sources. The psychic can then work to analyze the problems or choices their client is facing in order to give the best and clearest counsel.

It is the sensing and diagnosis of these energy flows that allows the psychic to receive and understand the subtle information present in and around the individual for whom they are performing a reading or psychic healing. By becoming consciously aware of any energy blockages challenging their client, and the locations of these blockages (whether within the physical system, the auric field, the mental perceptions, or emotional responses of the individual), the psychic can analyze, understand, and begin to counsel their client about ways that they can take control of and transform attitudes and situations of concern to them.

To begin to recognize and strengthen your sensitivity toward the acquisition of knowledge within energy flow patterns, practice the following exercises to learn the different flavors energy can express.

EXERCISE 1: SENSING AND RECOGNIZING THE FEELING OF ENERGY—MEDITATIVE BREATHING

Sitting in a comfortable chair outdoors, or in a sunny window, focus on the sensation of warmth you are experiencing that is emitted by the sun's rays. In your mind's eye, visualize the energy from the sun coming into your body through your conscious breathing. As you inhale slowly to a count of four, let this energy flow throughout your entire body—cleansing, soothing, and making each organ and individual cell glow. Then, as you slowly exhale your breath to a count of four, feel yourself releasing any stress, imbalance, and ill health. Let any imbalance or negativity leave your body with that exhaled breath. Continue to breathe slowly and with focus. With each inhalation, breathe in light and balance, with each exhalation release stress and imbalance. You may want to repeat a mantra inside your head as you breathe to help you stay focused. As you inhale, think "Light. Energy. Health." As you exhale, think "Release. Let Go. Relax." Plan to spend about five minutes performing this exercise. You have just washed every organ and cell in your body and your aura and you are now cleansed and refreshed.

EXERCISE 2: FOCUSED DIRECTIVE BREATHING

If you have a specific illness such as a stomachache or head-ache, direct the energy you are absorbing from the sun to the spot of physical discomfort in your body as you inhale slowly and with focus. Direct the incoming energy that you are access-ing via your focused breath to the afflicted area and hold the energy there for a few moments. Concentrate on what the sun's energy feels like within your body. Then, in your mind's eye, visualize the energy gathering and coalescing in the imbal-anced area. With focused thought, gather up any imbalanced energy in that spot. As you exhale slowly, visualize the gathered imbalanced energy in your mind's eye, and then release the energy of the illness along with your exhalation. You may find that as you do this, a particular color will come to mind. When you receive spontaneous information such as a color to use in your breath work, practice imagining that the breath you are inhaling and drawing into your body is tinted in that color or shade. Breathe it in and absorb the color into your cellular sys-tem, extending it into your aura as well, by imagining that your body is overflowing with this energy, and the color is radiating out through your skin and into the air surrounding your body.

Stand outside, barefoot, on the earth. Feel the grass and dirt under your feet. Smell the rich scent of Nature surrounding you. Become aware of the movement of the wind in the trees and sounds of bird calls and insects. In your mind's eye, imagine that you are sending down roots through your feet. Feel the slight tingling sensation as your own body's energy flow gathers at the soles of your feet in preparation for joining with the energy source of earth. With each inhalation, gather this energy and let it flow down to the soles of your feet. With each exhalation, let your energy roots burrow into the earth, seeking the earth's magnetic center. Perform each breath inhalation and subsequent exhalation ten times, or until you sense that your body from your·waist to your feet feels physically heavier. You can gently sway back and forth in perfect balance—the earth is providing grounding and is serving as a ballast for you. Once you have connected and rooted your energies with that of the earth, absorb energy from this rich source, just like a plant draws up and drinks water and minerals from the earth with its roots. As you inhale, drink up the earth energy through your roots. As you exhale, send feelings of love and thanks down through your roots to the earth. When you are finished, feel yourself drawing your roots back up into your body through your feet, using your breath. You will be calm, relaxed, and gently energized when you are finished. This is called Grounding and Centering.

EXERCISE 4: LIGHT ENERGY VISUALIZATION

Root yourself in the earth once again, this time just for balance. Don't absorb energy from this source. Instead, raise your arms above your head and draw energy from the air, sun, stars, or moon through the energy vortexes in the centers of your palms and through your crown chakra, located at the very top of your head. See and feel the energy, white, glowing, and radiant, flowing down from the sky into the palms of your hands, and with your focused breath, shoot this energy into every cell of your body. You will feel lighter, more uplifted, and your mind will be serene, open, and completely awake.

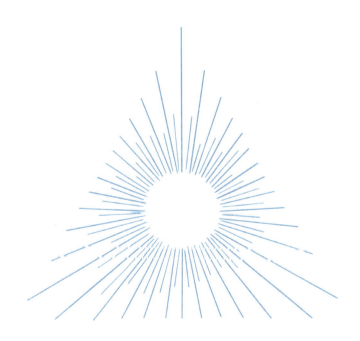

EXERCISE 5: PHYSICALLY AND PSYCHICALLY SENSING ENERGY

In this exercise you will work to create an energy ball by placing your hands in front of you, palm to palm, as if you are praying. Move the palms of your hands away from each other until they are about eight inches apart, and begin to do your focused energy breathing. After four or five focused breaths, very slowly bring your palms closer together. Let the palms approach each other, millimeter by millimeter, until you begin to palpably feel a slight resistance between your palms—as if they are being softly pushed away from each other. This is your own electromagnetic field, your aura, and you are sensing the force within it. When we get to Chapter 3, which focuses on clairvoyance and the other senses which correspond to our physical senses, we will be discussing some of the many things you can do with this energy. For now, your task is simply to continue to play with it as you hone your awareness and sensitivity to these feelings and sensations.

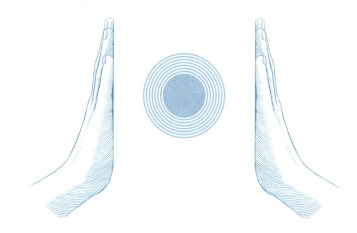

Use the energy ball palm technique from the previous exercise to energize your hands. Then, with your right palm about three inches above your skin's surface, begin slowly running your hand, palm side down, above one of your arms or legs. Open your senses and notice how the energy resonating from the limb feels. Is it smooth? Does it have a sensation that gives you the impression of cold or of heat? Does the energy above the limb feel constant as you run your palm through it, or are there areas where it feels like there are gaps or emptiness? You can do this exercise on yourself, but it is actually easier to experiment with a friend or colleague's body energy flows since you are so used to your body. When you work with a friend, you can make comments about the texture and quality of the energy you are feeling and get feedback about your psychic energy impressions. As you explore their energy, whenever you let your friend know that you notice a gap or a change in temperature in the energy pattern in a particular area of your friend's body and the auric field of that area, your friend may tell you of an old injury to that spot, or even begin recounting to you a story about an earlier emotional trauma. Difficulties or traumas that we have experienced in the past, but have not resolved, often settle into the energy pattern in a location in our body, waiting to be resolved and released. The emotional energy residue of the traumatic experience settling into a physical location is called a blockage and is part of the work that some psychics take on to release and heal the energy residue of that trauma.

What do you do with these energy flows once you have been able to feel them physically and psychically? You will begin to hone your skills at interpreting these flows and what kind of signals you are receiving on a psychic level from them. Does the energy feel hot to you? It could be an accumulation of vital force, which is either gathered to perform a specific function (healing or blocking), or as preparation for a release. Does it feel cold? This could be a break or tear in a person's auric field that is leaking energy, leaving the individual fatigued and susceptible to ill-health or stress. Do you get a color association with the flow when you feel it? As you pass your hands over the area, does a color spring to mind, or do you psychically see or feel a color? Part of your diagnosis of this energy color will be the type of expression associated with that color as well as your emotional response to it and any snippets of sudden psychic information or insight you receive when experiencing it.

One of the interesting things about psychic insight is how the information that is received sometimes has the action of a process called synesthesia. Synesthesia comes from the Greek *syn,* meaning "with" and *aisthesis,* meaning "sensation." This is when two of the body's physical senses pair up and trade sensory places in the way an experience is interpreted by an individual. This is the phenomenon that takes place when a person has the experience of tasting a color, smelling a musical note, hearing a number—when two or more of the senses entwine. Synesthesia is actually something commonly associated with newborn humans as they sort out how to interpret the various stimuli they receive to their physical systems. But synesthesia is also very common with the psychic senses. You may find that as you train your psychic abilities, when you read for others, certain types of energy always seem to come across to you as a green or a brown energy. You will learn then that when you encounter a flavor color of energy, its color denotes a certain quality or bit of data.

You can also use focused energy techniques to direct energy and intention into objects or places for energy storage purposes. You may wish to infuse your psychic reading room, your dream chamber, or your meditation space with a calm and clear flavor of energy to enhance and strengthen your work in those spaces. You may choose to give additional clarity and connection to the tools you use in your psychic work (tools such as a pendulum or divining rods) and to any healing tools you use to release or transform energy flow.

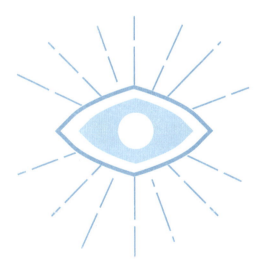

Ground and center yourself using the techniques in Exercises 3 and 4. If you are creating an intentional energy pattern in a space, you will first focus on what that energy should feel like. For a meditation space or a psychic reading room, you will want a feeling of calmness and serenity, of comfort and psychic cleanliness. After you are grounded and centered, you will focus on and visualize the color lilac (gentle wisdom) or light blue (peace), breathing in energy with your meditative breath and filling your body and aura with the color you have chosen. As you exhale, you will exhale this colored energy into the space. Continue doing this color energy breathing, filling your body and your aura each time with your inhaled breath and then radiating the color into the entire space with your exhaled breath. When you feel that the room has been cleansed and is full of this focused, colored energy, you will set the energy in place by clapping your hands once, ringing a chime, or stating "So shall it be" or another short phrase to that effect.

You want the kind of calm, focused energy that is discussed above in a space in which you are going to be doing psychic or energy healing work. But there are other uses for this technique as well. You can set a specific energy in a space for any purpose. Perhaps you are going to have a talk or a meeting with someone and you want to be sure that the communication is clear and honest and that both of you are receptive to each other's ideas. You would work as above, using pink (compassion) and light yellow (communication and comprehension) to infuse the energy of the room for the best results. Perhaps you have a child who has trouble sleeping at night. You would infuse the child's bedroom with the energy of light blue (peace) and white (purification) to help them relax into sleep and experience dreams that would be refreshing and restful.

If your intention is to direct energy into an object for a specific purpose, you would follow the methods as outlined previously, selecting the appropriate energy color for the object's purpose. Say that you wanted to charge a particular ring or necklace as a tool to help you open your psychic senses and be very clear about the information you obtain when you are meditating or performing a reading. The purpose of this piece of jewelry would be to help you more quickly access your psychic talents and analyze what you are getting. In this case, you would infuse the object with the energy color of medium purple (psychic wisdom), lilac, or pale blue. Perhaps you are training yourself as a medical intuitive or Reiki healer and wish to charge some crystal wands to help you move, transform, or release energy. After selecting your healing tools, you would infuse the tools for moving, dispensing, and transforming energy with the colors orange (vitality) and green (renewing) and the tools for drawing out and releasing energy with black (absorbing) and white (purifying).

You can also utilize focused energy to manifest your intended goals by psychically sending an intention out into the universe. If this is your desire, using the same energy techniques, you can focus, gather, direct, and release deliberate mental energy to manifest a goal via a purposeful meditation, prayer, or ceremony. Perhaps you would like to put the psychic message out there to meet like-minded, ethical individuals whom you could learn from and with whom you could share your knowledge and experience. Or perhaps you'd like to put out the psychic call to have the opportunities you need to grow in your spiritual and life's path open up to you. If you are seeking like-minded individuals, first determine what areas you are seeking to explore right now. Knowledge and ideas? Send a thought bubble out in yellow to attract individuals who have ideas and experiences that they like to share with other psychic seekers. Other healers? Send thought bubbles out in green, the color of healing and renewal. Opening more to your psychic gifts? Send lilac thought bubbles to attract those who are spiritually focused and psychically aware. Think about what your goal is and determine a short, concise sentence that encompasses your desire. Meditate on this thought, surround it with the color energy bubble, and let it float away.

The conscious manipulation and transformation of energy is also useful when you need psychic shielding in negative situations. You may also need to create a permeable shield that allows some energy flow when you are reading for others so that you receive clear information. When you create a permeable energy shield, you receive the psychic information that you need when working with another person, while being able to clearly differentiate between the psychic information, the emotional responses your client has regarding that information, and your own opinions about the matter. This permeable shield also ensures that any issues that your client is dealing with don't transfer their energy to you. Instructions for the creation of a permeable shield can be found in the next chapter. The reasons for consciously focusing energy, and the ways in which the manipulation and transformation of energy can be focused, are versatile, numerous, and applicable to every area of psychic work, energy healing work, and your daily life.

CHAPTER 2

Opening to Your Intuition: Building a Strong Foundation for Your Psychic Work

The "trick" to being psychic is very simple: you need to be able to hear and listen to your inner voice clearly in order to receive the information that is being offered to you via your psychic senses. Learning to meditate teaches you how to quiet your thoughts and center your focus and concentration so that your inner voice can speak clearly to you—and so that you are ready to listen. In addition, the practice of meditation teaches you how to enter the alpha brain wave consciousness purposefully. In the alpha brain state, your focus and awareness is on your internal experiences—feelings, intuitions, and creative thought, because your electrical brain wave patterns are moving at a slower frequency or rhythm.

Scientists and physicians who study the human brain have discovered that it generally produces brain waves in four basic classifications. *Beta*, our normal waking consciousness state when we are focused on tasks and memorization, exhibits brain wave frequencies between 12 to 38 Hz; *alpha*, the brain wave state humans experience during meditation and times of relaxed creativity with a frequency between 8 to 13 Hz; *theta*, the brain wave state we experience in between waking and sleep when we are just coming out of our dreams with frequencies between 4 to 8 Hz; and *delta*, when the brain is in a deep sleep or unconscious mode with frequencies below 4 Hz. Hz is the abbreviation for Hertz, which is a unit of frequency measuring the change in state or cycle of a sound wave, alternating current, or other cyclical waveform, in this case the electromagnetic activity of the brain, of one cycle per second.

Being in the relaxed alpha brain wave mode of consciousness allows you to have a clear bridge of communication between the right hemisphere of the brain—the place of creativity and psychic sensitivity—and the left hemisphere of the brain—the place of logic, linear thinking, and perceptions. Meditation and centering allows for a clear channel of communication between the two halves of the brain, which will bring you clarity, insight, and understanding of the psychic information you receive.

Now, when I speak about your "inner voice," keep in mind that you may get your psychic information in a different way than "hearing" it inside your head. Sometimes you may just get a flash of information and suddenly simply "know" something. You may have a vision that could be a complete scenario, or it may be simply a symbol or a face that you will need to work with as you interpret its meaning further. You may hear a quiet voice in your mind which gives you information. You may receive psychic information via your dreams. You may use a psychic tool such as the tarot or I Ching and interpret the cards or the throw of the coins. You may use a scrying mirror or crystal ball to psychically "see" scenes, images, symbols, colors, or numbers. You might employ a pendulum and use it to gain answers by the direction that it moves. There are many ways to obtain psychic impressions, intuit answers, and receive specific information that will help yourself or others.

When I use the term "inner voice," I am talking about accessing that part of yourself that receives, interprets, and recounts information not obtained from your everyday material world or physical senses. It doesn't matter the method by which you get the information or how it may be presented to you. The important point is that you pay attention and take note of the information that you receive.

Your inner voice is like any other part of you—the more you use it, the stronger and more skilled it gets at giving you information. The less you use it or pay attention to it, the more it atrophies and weakens. Everybody is a born psychic. You, me, everyone. It's a natural ability and a part of what it means to be human. Some people are born with such a strong inner voice that they can't help but hear it—these people, if not trained, may not be able to understand what they are getting, but the voice is strong. If they don't understand why they are having these visions or why they can feel emotions and thoughts so strongly from others, they might work hard to shut it down, but it will always be there, ready to communicate again. Learning to hear your inner voice is like learning to play an instrument, becoming skilled at a sport, or mastering anything. What you have to do is acknowledge the desire and then practice the discipline. And then practice some more. The more you practice anything, the more skilled you become. It's exactly the same with developing and honing your innate, human psychic skills.

The ability to meditate is essential to clearly hearing your inner voice. If you cannot quiet your mind, relax, center yourself, and focus, you will find that trying to access that inner voice and listen to what it has to tell you will be a frustrating experience. Sure, you'll still be able to get the occasional psychic "hit," but it will come sporadically, and I bet it will come when you are daydreaming or in that half-asleep, relaxed alpha brain state before you begin to drift into sleep at night or as you wake up in the morning. You will have a psychic experience at times when you are inadvertently in a slightly altered, quieter state of mind. If you want to use your psychic skills dependably and in a conscious way, you'll learn the basics of meditation.

Sometimes when people hear the word "meditation," they have the mistaken notion that they have to commit to a lengthy process in order to achieve a mental state of complete, total sublimation and control of the conscious mind. Not at all. No, you don't have to chant mantras or be able to keep your mind absolutely blank for ten minutes or more. I'm talking about creating a meditative state of mind wherein you are calm, relaxed, and receptive. A state where you can focus on just one thing for a few minutes at a time, allowing your quiet thoughts to examine that one thing, consider it, and explore it. As you do this, your breathing will naturally slow, your body will relax, and you will feel at great ease. This thing that you are focusing on can be an image, a question, a feeling, a sensation, or a concept.

EXERCISE 8: FIVE MINUTE BREATH MEDITATION

Try this: sit or lie in a comfortable position. Begin by focusing your attention solely on your breath. Pay attention to your breath as you inhale. Feel the air entering your body, filling your lungs, and let your body begin to relax. Then focus on your breath as you exhale that air. Feel it leaving your lungs and your body relaxing even further. Now, breathing in slowly through your nose, hold your breath softly for four counts. Breathe out slowly through your mouth. Don't breathe for four counts. Do this simple exercise for five minutes (I'd suggest putting on a timer so that you don't keep looking at your watch, thereby losing your focus). If you succeed in paying attention only to your breath, you have just meditated for five minutes. Do this exercise twice a day for two days. You don't need to make a big production out of it, but you do need to meditate on your breath at least twice a day. After you have done this exercise a few times a day for a week, you will know in your body what it feels like to be relaxed, you will know how it feels to be relaxed in your mind, and you will have the ability as you begin a focused breath how to instantaneously enter an alpha brain state.

EXERCISE 9: MEDITATION AND VISUALIZATION

The next step is to add a thought, a saying, a color, or an image to your focus as you breathe in to your slow, four-count rhythm. As you begin your breath, allow your focus to engage itself with a relaxing thought, a positive memory, your favorite color, or the image of clouds drifting in the sky. As you do your breathing for the next five minutes, casually examine that thought, relive that memory, breathe in your favorite color or watch the clouds drifting by in your mind's eye. You will find that as you examine the thought or relive a favorite memory, images will spontaneously come into your mind having to do with the thought or memory. This is a process called "visualization": seeing something within your mind's eye. Experience the focused relaxation in this exercise twice a day for two days. Now it is time to move on to the first step of developing a relationship with your inner voice.

Just like a person, your inner voice will stop speaking to you if you don't listen to it. Oh, it's still there, but there's no point in talking to you—you are ignoring it. If you have been oblivious to your inner voice for a length of time, you will need to re-initiate the dialogue with your inner voice. With this next exercise, you will begin the conversation.

Start by doing your meditative breath. A minute or so into that exercise, pose a random question to yourself, asking yourself the question inside your head. Then simply continue your meditative breath. Your question could be as simple as, "What is something I need to be paying attention to in my life?" Or perhaps you may be juggling a couple of job offers currently. Ask "Which job suits me the best?" Or you may just let your mind completely surprise you and ask a question that comes out of the blue. The important thing here is to ask the question and then continue the meditative breath. This gives your inner voice some space to answer you as you remain quiet, relaxed, and focused.

Pay attention to how you get your answer. Do you hear it inside your thoughts or outside of yourself? Do you receive a picture, a scene, a symbol, or an image? Do you get a feeling somewhere in your body that gives you your answer? Do you receive a scent that has meaning to you, or a taste that gives you information? Do you just suddenly know the answer to your question?

There are several ways you may receive your answer. You may see a picture in your mind that symbolizes the thing you need to be paying attention to, or the logo of the company that would be the better job offer for you to take. You may just suddenly have all the information that you needed in answer to your question—a quick flash of inspiration. You may hear that inner voice in your head as it gives you the answer. The scent you smell or the taste you experience may bring back to you

continued on the next page

continued from the previous page

a long-lost memory of something that is associated with your question, thereby giving you the answer.

Or, you may get nothing at all. If that happens, there is nothing to worry about or become frustrated over; the answer will typically come to you spontaneously in the next day or two. It may come in the next few days in a sudden knowing, through a vision, or in a quiet answer inside your head. Your answer may come in a dream or in that time when you are just awakening and your brain is moving into the alpha state after sleeping. This alpha state is the best state for psychic work and is part of what you are working to achieve by practicing meditation. The brain is awake, aware, and focused while being relaxed, creative, and receptive. What you want to develop for your psychic work is the ability to deliberately alter your mental activity and brainwave state to that of alpha or even the deeper theta brain wave state at will, and with intention.

Once you have psychically received a response to your question, the next step is to act on the answer. Letting your inner voice know that you have heard and understood it is important, but just as important is to acknowledge that information by doing something with it, or about it, and acting upon the wisdom you have received.

Each time you receive psychic information, acknowledge your inner voice, and then act on the information. In this way, you will find that the inner voice of your subconscious is encouraged to give you the answers that you are seeking and will be ready to interact with your conscious mind again. Each time you do this, your senses will be strengthened, and you will be working to develop the tool in acquiring information above and beyond your five physical senses—your sixth sense.

EXERCISE 11: GROUNDING AND CENTERING—CONNECTING YOUR ENERGY TO THE EARTH'S MAGNETIC FIELD

Grounding is a term used to describe the process of aligning your energy field with the energy field/aura of the earth, creating a strong connection and keeping an open flow between yourself and that power. The process is very simple. Unplug your phone, turn off any distraction like the radio or television (you can play some quiet, calming meditation or classical music in the background, however, if you like), and give yourself a few minutes when you will not be interrupted.

Sit comfortably and place both your feet flat on the floor, with your forearms and hands resting relaxed on the arms of the chair you are sitting in, or with your hands placed palms down on your thighs. Begin to breathe slowly and deeply to a count of four. Inhale to a count of four, hold, then exhale to a count of four. With each inhalation imagine that you are breathing in vitality, light, softness, and awareness. With each exhalation, imagine that you are exhaling any stress or imbalance. Breathe in . . . hold . . . exhale.

With your first inhalation, place your focus on the soles of your feet where they are resting on the floor, and the backs of

continued on the next page

continued from the previous page

your legs as they rest in the chair. As you breathe in vitality, light, softness, and awareness, begin to draw up energy into your feet like a plant drinks water. Exhale, relax your muscles further, and release any stress or imbalance. Inhale, drinking up the earth's energy and bring that energy into your legs up to your knees. Hold, then exhale, relaxing and releasing further. Inhale, drawing up the earth's energy, vitality, light, softness, and awareness again, this time up to your waist. Hold, exhale, relax, release. Inhale again, drawing up the earth's energy using your spinal column, this time up to your shoulders. Let it run down your arms to light up your hands. Hold, exhale, and relax. Inhale, drawing up the energy again, channeling it through your spinal column. Draw it up your back, into your neck, and then your head—feel the energy tickle across your scalp. Exhale. You are now connected to the pulse of the earth and your energies are centered. You can release any excess or negative energy through this connection by running the energy down your body's energy currents into the earth and rejuvenating yourself by drinking up more energy as needed. Your body will feel very relaxed. Notice that your body, particularly the lower half from the waist down, feels heavy and dense. You are grounded, and your energies are focused and centered for your work.

The first couple of times it may take you up to ten minutes before you feel completely grounded and at ease. As you continue grounding over time, you will find that you can do this exercise in less than a minute, simply by breathing in that first focused, intentional breath.

When reading for other people or psychically investigating the energy of an object or a place, you want to be sure that the information you receive is clear and unbiased. The emotions of your client may be strong—they may be troubled, grieving, depressed, or frightened, and that is why they have contacted you to read for them. You want to ensure that the psychic impressions and information you are accessing are correct, and not the result of the empathic psychic connection you have with your client. If you are reading the energy of a place like a deserted house, you want to be sure that the feelings you are getting are coming from the energy that resides there, not your own preconceptions about the place. After you have grounded your energies in preparation for your work, it's time to create your shield to ensure this clarity and understanding of the psychic impressions you are receiving.

EXERCISE 12: CREATING A PERMEABLE ENERGY SHIELD

Ground and center yourself with your breath. Begin drawing more earth energy up into your body. Expand your auric field and fill your body with the energy of the earth. Radiate this energy, letting it extend outside of yourself two to four feet in all directions: on all sides as well as above and below you. See in your mind's eye the exterior parameter of energy thicken slightly. It might look to your mind's eye like you are inside of an egg of light. Draw up a bit more energy with your focused breath and send it consciously to your diaphragm—your seat of vitality. With this focused breath, set the shield and prepare to do your psychic work. By "set the shield," I mean intentionally acknowledge that the shield is set firmly in place. You can do this by any type of signal to yourself: clasping your hands, stomping a foot, stating verbally, "the shield is set," any signal that has meaning to you. This will finish the energy shielding process.

As you psychically open to the energies and begin to read, keep your emotions as clear and positive as possible. When you are working with other people, their problems can be difficult to hear when they are particularly difficult and intense. Your job is to present the information to the person you are reading for with clarity as you help your client discover positive solutions to their problems. You will not be doing them a favor to simply tell them that everything is dire and send them on their way. Conversely, you will not be doing them any favors if you gloss lightly over the difficulties that they are facing. There are always solutions to problems—not always easy solutions, but solutions all the same. Since you know that by changing behavior patterns, emotional reactions, and ingrained thought patterns, a person can and will change the future, you need to share that certainty with your client and explore ways they can make the needed changes in order to solve the problems they are facing.

Creating Sacred, Serene, Clear Space for Psychic Work

In addition to being grounded, centered, and shielded while you exercise your psychic talents, you will find that creating clean, clear energy space within a room prior to doing psychic work is a good way to receive clear information. When you create sacred space in a room, you are clearing the energy in the space, removing any muddy, imbalanced, or distracting energies that may be present. In addition, you are filling the room with neutral energy, cleansed of any extraneous vibrations that may be counterproductive or jarring to the work you are about to perform. By clearing, cleansing, and sealing a space for your psychic work, the energy is calmed and centered, allowing you to also be calm and centered so you can interpret the information you are receiving accurately.

In most traditions, a space is cleansed and focused by working with the energies in the shape of a circle. It is in a circular motion that energy moves naturally in our universe. Just as our planet is round, it also rotates in a circular motion each day and moves in a circular motion around the Sun. Have you noticed that when you let the water out of your bathtub, the water swirls in a circle as it moves down the drain? This circular movement is the natural way that all energy, whether in physical or etheric form, moves.

The creating of sacred space can be as complex or as simple as you want it to be. The main components, regardless of the way you choose to do it, are that you lay out the size of your space, mark the perimeters, cleanse the interior, and take it down or release the energies at the end of your work. And if you are reading for different clients in different sessions, you will cleanse the space and set the energy between sessions, so that the concerns of a previous client will not be present to confuse your information as you read for another.

If the space that you are working in is quite large, you don't need to cleanse and purify the entire room if you will simply be sitting at a table or desk while reposing in a chair while you read for a client or for yourself. You can just purify the immediate vicinity, creating an energy bubble that extends a few feet beyond yourself, your client, and the furniture.

There may also be times when you want to actually read the energy of a room, building, or space. In this instance, you will create a bubble of cleared energy around yourself and your aura, so you can receive the energy impressions of the space, but still be centered, alert, and calm as you interpret the information you are receiving with clarity.

EXERCISE 13: SIMPLE SPACE-CLEARING TECHNIQUE

For the majority of the psychic work you will be doing, creating sacred space in a simple fashion is just fine. Begin by standing in the center of the space that you will be using, while connecting your energies with those of the earth just as you do in the grounding exercise. With steady, quiet breathing, draw up into your body the grounding, stabilizing energy of the earth and then project this energy from your solar plexus (diaphragm), while slowly turning in place clockwise until you have completed a circle around yourself. As you turn, visualize the energy flowing from you in a band of light, and project it far enough into the space to give yourself plenty of room. After you have completed your psychic work, stand again in the center of the space, turn slowly, and release the energy that has formed the perimeter of your circle back into the earth. This is a very simple act that you can perform anywhere you choose to open up psychically.

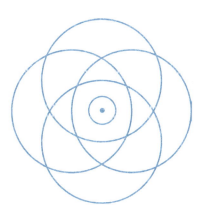

EXERCISE 14: FORMAL SPACE-CLEARING TECHNIQUE

Use this ceremonial, formal space-clearing technique when you will be involved in very intense psychic work and plan to be in deep trance.

You will need:

✧ Two tables

✧ One incense burner and incense

✧ Aromatic oil

✧ Charcoal

✧ Matches

✧ Bowl

✧ Chalice

✧ Salt

✧ Spring or distilled water

✧ One white candle, plus four more of any kind

✧ Psychic tools, such as tarot cards, a pendulum, or a scrying mirror (optional)

You will need two tables to organize your room: one at which to sit with your client, and one to hold your cleansing supplies (salt, water, bowl, chalice, and incense burner). Prepare to cleanse the space by assembling all of the necessary tools (your tarot cards, pendulum, scrying mirror, or whatever psychic device, if any, you are using that day) and an oil that you plan to utilize to open your psyche to information and impressions. Place these items on the table at which you and your client will sit. On a separate table, place an incense burner, charcoal, matches, sanctifying incense such as frankincense or sage, your cleansing supplies, and any odds and ends you want. Now, place the one white candle (called the flame candle) in the center of your cleansing supplies table and light it.

Determine the orientation of the room (where its northern, southern, eastern, and western regions are), and then set the table where you will be doing your psychic work in the westernmost part of the room, if possible. West is the direction of the element Water, the element of the subconscious mind, intuition, and emotions. Just prior to the cleansing, place a lit candle at the edge of your circle in the north, east, south, and west to represent the element of that direction or quarter.

North relates to the element Earth, the element of the physical plane, manifestation, and grounding. East relates to the element Air, the element of the conscious mind, knowledge, and communication. South relates to the element Fire, the element of conscious will, life vitality, and transformation.

You will begin by going to the north or east quarter of your circle. You will decide for yourself which quarter or direction you begin in—some people who practice a Nature-oriented spirituality begin in the north, to honor the earth upon which we live. Others who follow other western magickal traditions begin in the east, for it is there that the sun rises. Begin in whichever direction makes the most sense to you.

Stand there for a moment, slowing your breathing and sensing energy rising up into your body from the core of the earth. When you feel calm, centered, and comfortably full of energy, simply raise the arm that you write with (your active side) over your head, breathe in energy, and then gently drop your arm in the direction of the floor, sending the energy out of your hand as you create the perimeter, walking clockwise around the circle.

continued on the next page

continued from the previous page

Next, go to your table where you have placed your cleansing supplies and pour some spring or distilled water into the chalice, then add three or four pinches of salt (for the element Earth). Walk to the north or the east (wherever you started when you drew out your circle) and sprinkle the saltwater as you walk the perimeter of the circle completely, feeling the elements of Earth and Water cleansing the area and balancing it. If you wish to chant or say a prayer as your cleanse the circle, it can help you to concentrate and visualize the cleansing even better.

Return to the supplies table and light the charcoal in your incense burner with the white flame candle. Let the charcoal ignite completely, then drop a small amount of incense onto it (this can be the incense you like to use for opening psychically, or a traditional cleansing incense such as frankincense or sage leaves). Go to the same place in the circle where you began your cleansing, in the north or east, and gently waft the incense smoke in the circle as you walk the perimeter again with your incense burner. This represents the elements Fire and Air. Again, feel the elements of Air and Fire cleansing the area and balancing it.

Your sacred space is created, cleansed, and balanced. Now it is time to begin your psychic work.

When you have finished with your reading and your client has departed, it is time to release the energies that have created the perimeter of your circle. Go to the quarter in which you began (north or east), and either verbally or mentally thank the powers of that element for their balancing effects, while extinguishing the lit candle there. Do this at each quarter and, finally, extinguish the white flame.

Whew! Sounds like a lot to go through? This formalized cleansing would be appropriate for deep trance work, past-life work, or any type of intense work where you would be more or less in a very altered state of alpha consciousness for the duration of the experience.

CHAPTER 3

Clairvoyance and Other Techniques to Access Your Psychic Senses

The psychic sense of clairvoyance is the one most often associated with being psychic or intuitive, but there are other ways that psychic information may be received. In this chapter, we'll examine and explain them all, but we'll start with the one that is best known.

Clairvoyance

The term clairvoyance means "clear seeing" (*clair* meaning "clear," and *voyance* meaning "sight"). This technique is often used to read auras, or to interact with spirit guides to interpret the subtle energy patterns within, surrounding, and acting upon an individual. The experience of clairvoyance can be defined as a psychic connection wherein you receive the psychic energy present within a person or a situation in a visual manner. This experience can occur in your mind's eye, like the visions you have when you are daydreaming and you experience a picture or image in your mind. Or, the information can appear as an image, a person, or a scene outside of yourself, as if you are seeing it with your physical eyes. Actually, you are using your psychic "sight" to view the scene or image you are receiving.

In addition to images, people, or scenes, clairvoyant vision may also be made up of the energy colors present in the aura of someone or something that you are reading. The clairvoyant can also sometimes see the image or form of a spirit guide or angelic guide who is present. Clairvoyance is particularly associated with the Third Eye (the energy chakra center just above and between the eyebrows) as a method or talent to see images, symbols, scenes, and colors in the mind's eye that are present within the energy field around a person, place, or thing. When these images or colors are perceived clairvoyantly, the next step is to interpret their meanings.

BRAIN WAVE STATES

Alpha

A clairvoyant reading occurs when a psychic goes into a light trance state to obtain information and impressions through their subtle psychic senses. The psychic has engaged their mind in the alpha brain state—the time when the subconscious mind is active. In this state, your focus and awareness is on your internal experiences—feelings, intuitions, and creative thought. In an alpha brain wave state, your electrical brain wave patterns are moving at a slower frequency or rhythm (around 8 to 13 Hz) and your attention is alert to what is happening within yourself and your inner perceptions.

Beta

When you are functioning in your normally busy, day-to-day activities, your brain wave patterns are functioning in what is called a beta brain wave state, and your electrical brain waves are moving at around a 12 to 38 Hz frequency. The beta conscious mind state indicates that the brain is more concerned with the stimuli and activity outside of yourself, and those stimuli are being experienced and interpreted by your conscious, linear mind. The stimuli that your brain is responding to tend to be matters and experiences that are external to yourself.

As you relax into the meditative alpha brain wave state, you will begin to sense, understand, and diagnose the energy patterns of an individual, object, or place. You will be able to do all this while noting the visual input you are receiving from your intuition, as well as the feelings that the scenes, symbols, and images you are experiencing evoke in you. Clairvoyant visual imagery emerges as the energy patterns of a person or a thing are experienced by your subtle senses. You will find while using your clairvoyancy that, in addition to the colors, scenes, or images you are receiving, you will also be accessing various psychic impressions, bits of information, and messages from your other psychic senses as well. In addition to the clairvoyant experience, you may also feel sensations in your body, you may get a sudden knowing with the image or color, and words may pop into your head. The experience of clairvoyance is often accompanied by these other psychic senses as aid in clarifying and interpreting the visual image that is being received during your psychic work.

You may see a symbol and find that the symbol comes with a psychically audible message as in the experience of clairaudience. A clairvoyant vision may appear and, in addition, you may have the experience of claircognizance—where the image is accompanied by a sense of knowing additional information or having a psychic hit, which tells you exactly what that image means. Sometimes the vision may come with a physical sensation, called clairsentience, wherein you receive the image along with a physical feeling of emotional response from within yourself—happiness, dread, awakening. You may also experience a physical sensation within your body—you may feel a pressure or slight pain in an area of your body, which gives you information about an illness that someone is experiencing. You may feel, for example, the weight of a cape around your shoulders, which gives you information about a past life led by the person you are reading.

This intuition-based information is sometimes presented to you, the psychic, from your higher self, from your own spirit guide or guides connected to the client, or from the energy imprint of the client. You, as the psychic, will gather the information from all of the sources at your disposal, and then communicate to the client the scenes, images, feelings, or symbols and what they mean in terms of the client's life and concerns.

THE AURA

Seeing on a clairvoyant level is the ability to psychically see, feel, and interpret energy patterns as colors and mental pictures in the aura: the energy field around the body and surrounding environment of the client. The aura is the personal energy pattern of a person, and revealed within it are all of the reasons and motivations for their actions. Each person's unconscious mind, motivations, and feelings are readily revealed within their auric field. By looking at and sensing the aura, as you use your clairvoyant skills, you can see what is happening in a person's life on an energy level, and analyze what current or past events have a bearing in regards to their health, emotions, thought processes, and spiritual connections. This auric information reflects what is occurring with the person in their physical environment and how they are reacting to events in their lives, giving you clear indications of the future they are creating by their attitudes and responses to events.

Sometimes a clairvoyant image will present a scene or present information in a straightforward way, but the visions will not always be completely straightforward. Our psychic abilities originate, like our dreams, within the subconscious mind. The language of the subconscious tends to be in symbols—whether that symbol is a color, shape, image, or metaphor. And, like our dreams, which often present to us in allegory and metaphor, many times the clairvoyant message will need to be analyzed and interpreted to uncover the information it represents. For example, when reading for a person who is consulting with you regarding their relationship, if you receive a vision of them sitting in a small, cramped room, you may interpret that vision as their feeling trapped or confined in the relationship. If you receive a flash of yellow as you consider their question about the relationship, you may interpret that flash of color as an indicator of a shared intellectual and mental process between the two parties. Or, perhaps someone wants to know about how their new business venture will go, or how they fared during their coveted job interview. You may receive a psychic image of a champagne bottle and confetti—signifying success, celebration, and reward. You may receive an image of an automobile driving at a high speed up a road and coming to an abrupt stop as an official struts forward with some kind of form that requires a signature. This type of imagery would indicate a quick and seemingly effortless beginning for the project or job, but that not all of the details have actually been attended to and taken care of. Likely, success and reward can result if all the small details are accounted for, but there still needs to be attention given to making sure the situation is completely worked out.

When using your psychic senses to respond to a specific circumstance or question of concern to you or the person you are reading, it is easy to place and understand the images and psychic feelings you are accessing because you have a framework or focus to concentrate on. But there will also be times when you will experience a spontaneous clairvoyant vision. When you receive a clairvoyant vision out of the blue, it will not always mean something specific to you. Usually a clear and meaningful vision will occur at a time when you are deliberately seeking psychic information. But there are those instances when the energy residue surrounding a person, place, or thing is so strong that you receive the psychic information without seeking it deliberately. If you receive an unexpected clairvoyant image that has a strong emotional charge to it, but you are unable to interpret it immediately, try first relaxing and simply opening up your other psychic senses to troll for additional information. If, after a few minutes, the meaning of the vision is still unclear, file it gently in the back of your mind and go on with your day. You will very likely receive additional information via your dreams or in a sudden a-ha moment as you move throughout your day if it truly has significance for you.

Sometimes the term clairvoyance is used interchangeably as a descriptive word for the other types of psychic senses that we have. We can access psychic information in many ways and not just through clairvoyant visions. We can also use the subtle energy senses associated with our physical senses in our psychic information gathering.

Clairaudience

Clairaudience is clear-hearing, when the psychic receives information that comes to them with the perception of having been spoken to them as a single word, a sentence, a message or as a teaching. This psychic hearing sensation can feel as if it is inside your head or outside your ears, and can seem to you as if it is being spoken aloud, although no one but you can hear it. Oftentimes clairaudience is associated with having a guide—a disembodied spiritual teacher or mentor who gives you guidance and advice. You may receive a single important word, a sentence, a song, or a simple sound. Often, when all you get is a sound, it is a nudge to pay particular attention to what is around you and the feelings you have at that particular moment in time. It can be a signal that your guide is about to interact with you, or that you are about to encounter a person or experience that will have particular meaning or significance for you. You may sometimes find that you have a dominant ear for clairaudience, and that when you receive psychic information it seems to come always to your right ear or to your left ear. Most clairaudients report that their dominant ear is on the same side of their body as their dominant hand.

I have a technique that I find very helpful when I am using clairaudience to get the answer to a question. Typically what I will do is think briefly about something I would like to know as I get into my car to drive somewhere. I don't spend time meditating on the question, nor do I concentrate and ask myself the question over and over. I simply say the question aloud or think it to myself as I sit down and put my key in the car ignition. Then I drive to my destination. Sometimes during the drive, I will get an almost immediate answer; at other times the answer may not come for a day or two. But when I am driving again or engaged in another habitual task that does not require me to focus on things in a totally linear fashion, I will clairaudiently hear the answer—and the answers have all been right so far!

Clairsentience

Another way that you can access psychic information is through a process called clairsentience. The word clairsentience means "clear-feeling." One of the ways that clairsentience is used and experienced is by touching or holding an object as you open your subtle senses to psychically feel and interpret the energies attached to that object. This interpretation of the vibratory energies of objects is often referred to as psychometry. You can also experience clairsentience within your own body as you perform a psychic reading. You have heard the term "gut feeling." This term is used to indicate an intuitive hunch about someone or something, but when using your clairsentient talents this feeling can often be a literal one. You may experience the feeling of dread in your stomach, your stomach literally feels heavy and constricted, as you handle an object or read for an individual. You may experience an excited feeling, like butterflies in your stomach, as you psychically read something or someone. You may experience the hair on your arms literally rising, a sudden flash of cold or heat, or a prickling sensation in your aura or on an area of your body. All of these sensations can be clairsentient signals of psychic impressions that you are receiving. When this happens, also take note of any emotional responses you are having while the clairsentient sensation is occurring. Your emotional response will give you additional information and clues to help you interpret the meaning of what you are receiving.

Here are a couple of ways you can play and experiment with your clairsentient abilities. First, have a friend lend you a piece of jewelry or a picture that they have information about but that you don't. Relax and open your senses while you handle the jewelry or picture and let it begin telling you about the person or people who own or owned it. Relate the impressions you are getting to your friend and get their feedback.

You could also try going to an antique store or a garage sale. Pick up an object and feel the energy still residing within it. Ask the antique dealer or garage sale family after you have gotten your psychic impressions about the object and its origins for confirmation about the information you have received.

Claircognizance

Claircognizance is another way of obtaining psychic information and the term means "clear-knowing." When you experience claircognizance you suddenly know certain things without being told about the situation or person. This information can be provided to you by your higher self, that part of you which is intimately connected with your subconscious mind and the Divine, or by your spirit guides as they provide you with information in the form of thought into your mind and awareness. This knowing can be in the form of a simple word or sentence, or it can be an entire body of information that you receive into your consciousness. You may receive a sudden inspiration or idea that is new to you, or you may experience a small insight about someone or a circumstance. When you experience claircognizance it will be characterized by a very strong sense of correctness about the information you are receiving. Sometimes this knowing will be accompanied by a clairvoyant vision, but more often it comes as a sudden flash of clear knowledge which just feels right. Claircognizant experiences come with a feeling of rightness and certainty. When you receive psychic information in this way, you do not have any doubt of the veracity of the information.

In addition to receiving knowledge about something or someone in your mind, you may also experience claircognizance when you engage in the psychic activity of automatic writing. In the process of automatic writing, you place yourself in an alpha brain wave meditative state with the intention of receiving psychic information. Using pen and paper or a computer word processing program, you open your psychic senses and allow yourself to channel, or bring through, information not previously known to you while in a light trance state.

You may wonder: if the experience of claircognizance comes in the form of thoughts or words, how can you tell if what you are getting is a psychic hit, or if it is really just your own thoughts? The claircognizant knowing comes to you without your own thinking processes—the thought or information is suddenly just there. You have not engaged your conscious mind in obtaining the information and it has not been generated by your thought processes. When spontaneous claircognizance occurs, you have typically been using your conscious mind to think about something entirely different—the knowing you receive has nothing to do with what you were occupying your mind with the moment before.

You can begin to develop your skills at claircognizant knowing by engaging in meditation practice. As you relax into your meditation, focus your intention on opening up to the wisdom and knowledge within the universe. You may want to place your awareness particularly at the top of your head—at your crown chakra. I like to visualize a light at the top of my head glowing and shining brighter and brighter. Within this light, I imagine butterflies flittering, and each time one alights on my head, I receive a bit of inspiration.

Clairvoyance, clairaudience, clairsentience, and claircognizance are the four psychic senses that tend to be employed the most in intuitive work, but you also may experience clairolfaction, the psychic sense of smell, or clairgustance, the psychic sense of taste. When working with a guide, for example, one of the signals you may receive before psychic contact can be a scent: roses, a forest glen, the smell of ozone. You may also experience psychic smell when working to contact someone who has passed. You may get a whiff of their favorite perfume or their pipe tobacco smoke as you make contact, for example. The experience of clairgustance may occur under a similar circumstance when you are making a spirit contact with someone and suddenly taste some sort of food or drink that was particularly enjoyed by that individual during their life.

The Colors of Clairvoyance

Colors often accompany clairvoyant sight. When the color is clear and bright, its most positive aspects are being indicated. Murky or extremely pale shades of color tend to show the presence of that color's energy vibrations, but that those vibrations are weak or being used in an unbalanced fashion. The basic meanings of color vibration follow.

RED

Red is the color of physical life and vitality, sensual experience, and materialism. It is the slowest rate of vibration in which an animate form can exist in the physical world. Red's positive aspects are energizing, vitalizing, and heating. Red indicates the instinctual, animal nature. A clear, vibrant red will indicate physical vitality and energy. A pulsing red can indicate a blockage and irritation in the area where you are sensing the color. The negative aspects of red are destruction, discordance, and the shattering of physical form. The densest of the colors, red creates the most friction, which can attract or repel. Depending on the clarity or tint of the red in the aura, this color can indicate worries or obsessions, anger or brooding, anxiety, irritation, or nervousness.

ORANGE

Orange is the vitalizing color of the sun. This color is used by every living thing, inhaled by animals from the atmosphere through the lungs or gills. Plant life uses photosynthesis to take in and absorb the healthy color of orange. Orange combines physical energy with mental activity, unifying body and mind. Orange is the creative, preservative, regenerating force between matter and the higher faculties. Its positive aspects indicate thoughtfulness and consideration, while the negative aspects indicate laziness and repression.

YELLOW

Yellow governs the intellectual side of life, showing powers of reasoning, analysis, logic, and judgment. The true primary yellow is the highest color vibration on the planet, but is not visible to physical sight. It indicates the spiritualized, creative, illuminated intellect. Positive aspects of yellow show mental alertness and intellectual power. Negative aspects indicate timidity and weakness of will.

GREEN

Green is the color of growth, balance, and abundance. It shows the beginning of individual growth, the development of the ego and its sense of self. Green has strong healing vibrations and is the ray of finances and material wealth. It is the color of the lower, objective mind. It is the most difficult color for the clairvoyant to see and the last one to be seen clearly as clairvoyance develops. Green indicates a connection to, and love for, people, animals, and nature. It is the color of the teacher and healer.

BLUE

Blue is the color of spiritual power, higher mental faculties, and the subjective mind. It is inspirational, devotional, spiritual, soothing, cooling, and harmonizing. Positive aspects of blue are spiritual connection, artistry, selflessness, and high morality. Negative tones of blue indicate struggle and melancholy. The luminescent, deeper tones of blue have great power, indicating that the individual has found their life's path and is dedicated to service. It is the color of the sensitive, intuitive person.

INDIGO

Indigo is the combination of blue with a small amount of clear red, which intensifies its power. It combines the deep blue of devotion with clear logical thought and action. Indigo indicates universality and a high degree of spirituality which unites spirit with matter. The positive aspects of indigo show intensity of purpose and the seeking of spiritual fulfillment and truth.

VIOLET

Violet is a bluish purple and is a pure blue with additional higher vibrations of pink within it. Violet indicates a lofty spiritual consciousness and great spiritual power. People with indigo in their energy field can raise their vibratory rate to that of violet if they work to keep themselves grounded and use their psychic abilities in a balanced, helpful way. This is a color indicating spiritual awareness and intuition.

Being psychically sensitive to color in the aura via clairvoyance is a helpful gateway to quick psychic analysis. But you may be one of those people who doesn't psychically *see* color but instead read the energies present in the aura through another of your psychic senses.

You may experience the energy present in the aura through the medium of clairaudience by psychically hearing information about the energy. Perhaps you obtain the information via clairsentience, meaning you experience the energy flavor of an individual, place, or thing as a feeling within your own body and use your senses to interpret that feeling. Or you might use your claircognizant abilities and instantaneously know the answer to the question being asked.

Although many people tend to see color clairvoyantly and go on to interpret its meaning from that psychic sight, not everyone receives their psychic impressions in that specific manner, so don't discount the psychic information you receive if it comes to you via a different psychic experience. The color seen and interpreted by the use of clairvoyance is only one way of assessing the energy flavor—play to your strengths and use your most natural talent as you develop your psychic senses.

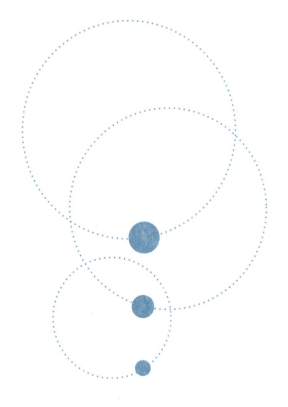

CHAPTER 4

Contacting Spirit and Angelic Guides

There are many energy beings available and willing to help guide human spiritual development with advice, information, answers, and helpful, subtle psychic nudges. These beings are commonly called guides, and can be from various levels of energy existence and can appear to you in many different forms. Their guidance and help is usually unobtrusive and delicate—you receive a sudden inspiration about the way to solve a problem, or you synchronistically run into someone who knows exactly the right person you need to talk to who can help you. A guide may contact you to give you some specific help at a time of need. You may not even be aware that this help has occurred; you just know that the problem you were facing has been mitigated or solved.

Once you become consciously aware of your guide or guides, your interaction with them will become a two-way street. When you are aware of their existence and the aid that is out there for your asking, you can deliberately set up a time to make contact with them to ask for any help that you are seeking. They will help you take care of difficulties; offer you guidance for your next step in your spiritual development; let you know what action will be the most effective and efficient in attaining a goal; offer you ideas to expand a creative project you are undertaking; help to give you strength and self-discipline; or aid in your psychic development. Whatever you are working toward, the help of a guide is always available to you. Once this relationship has been established, you will become more sensitive to, and aware of, their presence and their hand in helping to guide your life. You can consciously utilize their wisdom to make the best decisions in a situation and take the most fruitful actions, which will lead quickly to the results you desire.

A guide can be of angelic origin or from one's own ancient ancestral heritage. A guide can also be in the spirit form of a departed relative or a friend who has passed away. A guide can serve as a teacher or mentor to you, helping inspire your creativity. Or one may work as a guardian to you and your family.

Spirit energy forms that are commonly called "light beings" are different than guides. While guides are concerned with the development of an individual, a light being is concerned about the healing and evolution of the planet. Light beings will work to raise the spiritual consciousness of a group, a community, a country, or the planet as a whole. While they may choose, as part of actualizing their purpose, one or more individual humans to act on their behalf in the planet's evolution, the goal of a light being is to affect the planet in its entirety, not just one individual. The humans that a light being chooses to help them in raising the entire consciousness of a community, nation, or the world will be those people who have a natural knack for communicating with large groups of people and inspiring them—authors, political or religious leaders, community organizers—individuals who have a natural talent for leading, inspiring, and galvanizing other folks to take action. This interaction with a light being can sometimes result in the life of the human who has been selected to partner in this work to have their personal lives changed dramatically for that lifetime and sometimes for lifetimes to come.

A spirit guide typically has been close to humanity either through millennia of experience and interaction with humans or was once human in form themselves. They have an understanding and sympathy with the way that humans think, feel, and act, and their help tends to be given with the understanding of how humans function. A light being has a mission and a purpose—the spiritual evolution of a planet, a community, a galaxy—but they do not have emotions or an understanding of the limitations that a physical body can have.

The concept of spirit guides who are available and willing to help us is not limited to the work of mediums, psychics, or spiritualists here in the Western world, but is also found in many cultures and beliefs the world over. For example, the people of the Amazon in South America, the Aborigines of Australia, and some Native American tribes believe in and communicate with spirit helpers and plant spirits as part of their ancestral spiritual traditions. In these indigenous cultures, these helpers are typically the spirits of their ancestors, or may be nature spirits that reside in a particular geographical area. In some areas, the helpers are totem animals associated with their village or tribe—animal spirits such as the eagle, dragonfly, or bear. In our urban Western population, one finds people who channel (bring through information) from angels, light beings from other dimensions, spirits who were once in human form but have passed away, as well as other spirit entities.

Everyone has at least one guide ready to work with them to help in their spiritual development, to divert danger, and protect them or help them make decisions about events in their lives. These guides watch over each of us in our mundane and our spiritual activities, and try to gently steer us in the right direction with their guidance—direct and indirect.

You have had a strong gut feeling—an intuition or psychic nudge that made you feel that you really needed to take a particular action or avoid taking an action—probably more than once in your life. That feeling or urge often comes when your spirit guide (some people like to call them a guardian angel) is lending you assistance through gentle psychic taps to awaken your attention to something that is about to take place. When you feel that nudge, it is still up to you to decide to act upon or to reject those intuitive feelings and the guidance coming from your spirit guide. A guide cannot, and will not, force or compel you to do anything. When you get that gentle psychic nudge, it is your job to pay attention, while using your psychic and common senses in your decision-making process to determine if you wish to act upon that nudge, and in what ways you wish to respond.

Many people go through their lives unaware of these spirit helpers on a conscious level, often only willing to listen to a guide when a tragedy occurs or when they feel lost and afraid. But why not actively engage with a guide who wants to help you along your path in the general course of your life and not just when you feel helpless? When you decide to deliberately and consciously be open to help from your spirit guide, you will find that the guidance offered is very clear about the matter being addressed. You still have free choice and free will to act upon the guidance or not, but you will know exactly where your attention and focus should be placed and what options are available to you.

Humans find that as our spiritual awareness strengthens and increases we tend to attract spirit helpers around us. You may be told who your guide is by another psychic or intuitive. Sometimes this introduction to your guide is a simple, general description about what they are there to help you with. Sometimes you will receive a physical description of the being as well as their name. It is when you begin to develop your own psychic skills that you will truly become aware of your guides and will be able to consciously and purposefully partner with them in your own development while taking advantage of the wisdom, protection, and guidance that they can offer. Spirit guides are concerned with your personal and spiritual growth, but their interaction and help in the physical world leads to their own evolutionary growth as well.

A spirit guide is a teacher, healer, or counselor who is in energy or spirit form. They are there simply to guide, not as an entity to whom you give your decision-making power. A true spirit guide never tries to take control of the life of the person with whom they are connected. You always retain your free will to act or not act upon the guidance. A guide cannot force you to do anything that you don't want to do, and in no way will try to dominate, intimidate, or control you. Working with a guide does not free you from the responsibility of your decisions and actions, and the guide is not the responsible party if you make the wrong decision—you determine what actions you will take as you steer your way through your life. Guides will help to lead you in the right direction, but ultimately the decision still lies with you. If a spirit guide has a negative influence on your behavior, or if you feel that they try to compel you to follow their directives, then the chances are good that it's not a spirit guide at all, but what is called a "lower astral entity form." Guides are there to offer you help, protect you, watch over you, and guide you in your life's path, not control or manipulate you.

While many people have one ongoing guide who is connected with them throughout their lifetime, you can also occasionally have an additional guide who may help you at different intervals during your life. A guide can come into contact with you at a particular time in your life when you are having difficulties, such as an illness or a crisis, to help you in solving that specific problem. A guide will sometimes appear to teach you about a certain thing that you need to pay particular attention to in order to actualize your life's path. You can also have more than one guide at a difficult time, each one assisting you with a specific purpose during a crisis. For example, you may have one guide who helps you with energy healing, and another guide who is working to protect you while your energies are low during an illness. You may have one guide who helps steer you toward understanding spiritual principles, and another who watches over you and your family. Some people meet their guides at an early age and that guide will stay with them until the end of this lifetime or incarnation. When children tell a parent that they have someone that no one else can see and who helps them with things or plays with them, we tend to call that unseeable someone their invisible friend, but in many cases it is the child's guide.

There are spirit helpers who may be known or unknown to you, who seek to aid you during certain challenging events during your life, although it may not always be obvious to you at the time. But if you listen to your gut feeling, or suddenly have an innovative idea or new thought that you have never considered before, you may have been listening to your guide or helpers in spite of yourself.

It is helpful to discover who your guides are so that you can choose to consciously open to their assistance. But you do need to keep in mind that not every energy being you encounter has your best interests at heart. Occasionally, a person makes contact with a being that they initially believe to be a spirit guide, but is in actuality a lower astral entity form. This is an energy being that has come into existence through the coalescence of negative energy wave patterns such as the emotions of ongoing fear or envy. As this entity comes into its own form of consciousness, becoming aware of itself and its own developing personality, it seeks to become an energy parasite on any unaware individual, feeding upon and consuming the individual's life force and vicariously participating in physical form experiences through contact with that individual. This can happen to people who are drug addicts or alcoholics, and to people who suffer from ongoing deep depression. It can also happen to naïve people who play with psychic tools like Ouija boards without taking the proper precautions, or to people who go into a place where a lower astral entity form has taken up residence, such as a deserted house. When the lower astral energy form comes into contact with an unaware and weak person, it will attach itself to the auric field of that individual and remain there until the entity is removed from the individual's life force field.

How do you know if the entity that has contacted you has intentions to be helpful, or if it is actually a lower astral level entity? Pay attention to the way the guide interacts with you and what their expectations and motivations seem to be. Note how you feel during and after contact—happy, alert, and comforted? This is a guide. Agitated, tense, and exhausted? This is evidence of a lower astral energy form. Confident and clearer on what you need to do? This is a guide. Confused and concerned that what you've been advised to do seems strange? This is the feeling you will get with a lower astral energy form. If the contact does not feel good, do not participate any further in communication with the entity.

Here are some of the ways that you can determine that the guide who you are communicating with is not a true guide but an entity masquerading as a guide.

1. There is a sense of jealousy about the way the guide wants your relationship to be—you are told to stay away from friends and family and that you are not to attempt to develop communication with any other guide.

2. The guide becomes angry if you ever question the information you are given.

3. You are instructed by the guide to do things that are dangerous to yourself or others.

4. You are the only one the guide will ever talk to and the information being given to you is not helpful, logical, or verifiable.

5. Your pets become nervous or tense and engage in strange, hostile behavior around you. Animals are very sensitive and are easily aware of energy forms who do not feel right to them, just as they sometimes react with hostility when they encounter a human being who is negative or dangerous.

6. Plants in your home become stressed and die. Just as your life force (prana, chi) can be preyed upon by a lower astral entity, living plants can have the life force sucked out of them by lower astral entities as well.

7. You are told by this guide that you are under attack by other people or by something in the spirit world and that only this guide can protect you.

8. You become sexually obsessed. Lower astral entities feed on energy provided by the life force of people, animals, and plants. Sexuality is a potent reservoir of energy, and a lower astral entity may influence you to engage in ongoing sexual acts to provide food for its existence.

9. You feel fatigued, confused, and depressed for more than a few days—you feel that sleep does not really give you any rest. You have recurring dreams within a short time period that are disturbing.

10. You have a strong, though vague, uneasy feeling and find it hard to fall asleep.

11. You seem to be very susceptible to all passing colds, stomach flus, and the like for a long period of time. You eat well, take your vitamins, get plenty of sleep and exercise, but your immune system seems to be shot for no reason and you can't keep your physical strength up.

12. There are unpleasant smells in your home that you can't find the source for and that, often, only you can smell.

13. You are usually a well-organized person, but suddenly your keys or important papers start going missing, and these disappearances continue to happen very regularly.

14. Lights go off and on in your house, your cell phone loses its address book for no apparent reason, electrical appliances begin going haywire.

If you experience some of the warning signs above, this can be a sign of a connection with a lower astral energy entity. What do you do to break this parasitic connection? The first and perhaps most important thing is to understand that as a human in physical form, you have the ultimate advantage—you are a creature of spirit *and* physical form, with all the strength and tools you need to break the connection. So don't feed the negative energy of fear to the entity who is trying to usurp your decision-making ability and your personal power. Lower astral entities feed on negative emotions, and the emotion of fear can be very powerful. If you allow yourself to simply indulge in feelings of fear and helplessness, instead of working to break the connection, you are continuing to provide energy to the entity, making the breaking off of the energy link between you and the entity more difficult. If you encounter any of the warning signs above, refer to Chapter 10, "Psychic Etiquette, Hygiene, and Troubleshooting Tips."

A true guide knows that a big part of human spiritual evolution is the development of discernment, self-discipline, and the understanding of the spiritual rhythms of the universe. It is in this way that we humans cultivate what is called the true will—that part of ourselves that is in harmony with the spiritual workings of the universe. The true will of a person seeks to help bring balance and union between the physical world and the world of positive spirit. When a person follows their true will, difficult issues and their positive resolutions become very clear, and opportunities open up before them with ease and a feeling of a natural path. The people who come into our lives are of a like nature to us, and help us follow our own spiritual path with their example, their ideas, and their support.

A guide seeks to help you fulfill your life's purpose, thus allowing you to make a real and positive contribution to the quality of life of the people you meet, and to our planet's evolution as well. Whoever the guide is, and from whatever background they come, they will have some form of natural affinity with you. It is this affinity and sympathetic energy that bonds you with your guide and allows you to work closely together. You will find that in your work together, a guide will not communicate with you in a lofty and ponderous style—information and ideas will be given to you with compassion and sometimes with humor. So don't be shocked when some of the help and information you receive is given to you with warmth and wit.

Initially our expectations of how we communicate with spirit guides can be confusing. Many times our expectations are based on what we think we know from movies or television shows, all of which tend to present the events in the program very dramatically in order to provide an entertaining story. In most cases, spirit guide communication is much less dramatic than how it is depicted in movies. It tends to be a subtle contact that, in most cases, you will need to be quiet and centered within yourself to fully recognize and experience. Spirit guides, regardless of which type they may be and what form they may take, are composed of energy that is less dense than physical form and is moving at a higher, faster vibratory rate than that of physical human form. Their style of communication can be very subtle—through dreams, omens, or a sudden thought or vision which just seems to pop into our heads.

Once we are skilled at spirit guide communication and have conscious awareness and contact, we are able to ask direct questions and receive direct answers. These answers are experienced most often as a sudden thought, image, or answer within our mind or in our general awareness. When we experience thought energy from a spirit guide, it can sometimes leave us wondering if the thought was ours alone, or if it was true communication from a guide. How do you tell the difference? When you are receiving information and advice from a spirit guide, the thoughts will sound like your own, but they will tend to be of better clarity, have more structure, and be more eloquent in style than your usual way of thinking or speaking. Once you have experienced dialogue with a specific guide, you will recognize their voice, the feeling of their energetic presence, and the way they present information to you as being uniquely the communication style of that particular guide. Sometimes, before directly communicating with you, a guide will announce their presence by a particular pleasant scent—a scent of a pine forest, the perfume of a rose. Or you may hear a bell gently tinkle, or a musical note sound. You may feel an energy buzzing by your body or head. These are signals to you to stop and pay attention.

When you still and center your mind—through meditation, the grounding of your energy, and focused breathwork—you will be able to detect, experience, and understand the thoughts and information being shared with you by your guide clearly. When you receive guidance from your guide, you are always free to ask questions for clarification and see what additional thoughts, feelings, or signs come to you. You also need to be patient as you receive information and guidance. Your spirit guide will be working with you, but in their own way and with their own understanding, not yours. They will sometimes wait for you to remove doubts, fears, blockages, and distractions that might undermine the use of the information they are working to give you. If you try to rush to develop the relationship with your guide, you will find that you are getting in your own way. Relax . . .

You may have heard or read about guides, but were not aware of the various differences in the types of guides (or the way that we humans perceive and interact with them) and the way they may contact you. There are many ways that a connection with a guide can be experienced. You may already have a guide who has contacted you and with whom you have an active relationship. Listen to their guidance and know that you have been blessed to have this contact. If you would like to have this help in your life, you can initiate contact by being open and actively seeking the connection. Always do this type of work in a psychically and physically clean space (see Chapter 2 for how to create a clear energy space).

With the following exercises, we will begin to explore the various types of guides and the different ways to make contact with them. Regardless of the type of guide with whom you would like to create a link and a relationship, the beginning steps will be the same.

EXERCISE 15: GROUNDING AND LIGHT VISUALIZATION

Regardless of the type of guide you intend to work with, you will always start with this exercise. Begin your work to make the psychic connection by starting at a time when you know you will not be interrupted. Unplug the phone, contain the household animals, go to the bathroom. Eat only lightly before your opening meditation and wear comfortable, loose-fitting clothing. Have a blanket or sweater on hand, as you might get slightly chilly when doing this type of psychic work.

If you have noisy neighbors or barking dogs near your meditation space, you may want to have some gentle, quiet instrumental music on in the background as a barrier against distracting noise. If you would like to burn incense or scented candles to add to your meditative state, the scent of jasmine, frankincense, or sandalwood would be appropriate.

Begin with a prayer or invocation asking for protection and guidance. Ground your energies and center your mind. Take some slow, deep breaths, calming your whole body, until you feel your heartbeat begin to slow and become synchronized (in rhythm) with your breath. Next imagine a brilliant white light in your mind's eye. Gaze at this light as it gets larger and brighter; feel how comforting and pure it is. Begin drawing the light towards you as if you were a magnet for this light. Bring the light into your breath and allow it to warm and comfort your heart. Allow it to enter your body with your inhaling breath and feel It expanding throughout your body and your mind. Feel the light becoming one with you as it fills your entire being,

continued on the next page

continued from the previous page

touching you, merging with you, and becoming a part of each of your individual cells from head to toe.

This exercise will open your senses and prepare you for contact with a guide. You will be relaxed and alert and your auric energies will be working at a higher, more subtle energy frequency, allowing the contact to be clear and easily maintained.

Ancestral Guides

Sometimes a guide will appear as an ancestral guide. This is a guide who has a kinship with you through your bloodline—perhaps a recently deceased relative or a family ancestor, no matter how distant. An ancestral guide can also be someone you have known in a previous lifetime who has not yet reincarnated and is willing to help you.

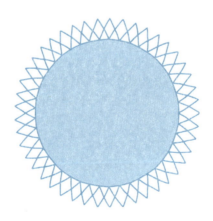

EXERCISE 16: CONTACTING AN ANCESTRAL GUIDE

Begin with the breathing and light visualization in Exercise 15 to open your senses and prepare yourself. Next, as you begin to create a contact and dialogue with an ancestral guide, start by meditating on the attributes of the potential guide. If you think you already know their identity, gaze at a picture of them if you have one and meditate to rekindle memories of that person—things you did together, things they said to you or did for you that enriched your life, the affection and love you have for that deceased individual. If you have access to a piece of clothing or jewelry once owned by the ancestor, meditate while holding this object.

If you don't know the identity of an ancestral guide, but are seeking connection with a guide who shares your genetic past, either through an actual family bloodline or through the bloodline of your general ancestry, start by reading some history of your ancestral heritage. Remember family stories about your genetic bloodline and the individuals within the family history's past as you meditate on their talents and successes.

During your meditation, you may begin receiving a subtle, initial contact. This contact can come in the form of a mild, physical, tingling sensation around your head or in your stomach area; a simple knowing when you are gently aware that the guide is in your presence. The contact can come in a clairvoyant seeing when you can psychically discern their form, color, or appearance. This contact can also come as a conversation

continued on the next page

---

continued from the previous page

in your mind with that individual ancestral guide. As you communicate with this guide, you are free to speak your questions out loud or to ask questions within your mind, whichever feels the most comfortable and natural for you.

Ascended Masters

Another form that a guide may assume is that of the ascended master. An ascended master's primary focus is to help all of humanity evolve spiritually. Ascended masters are typically associated with a particular spiritual path or mystery tradition and tend to interact more with groups than with just one individual. Mystery traditions are those traditions or groups that have had as their focus, throughout history, the spiritual evolution of the planet through training of individuals in spiritual techniques such as meditation, magic, psychicism, spiritual philosophy, and the like. The Western mystery traditions were developed through inspiration from various Western spiritual philosophical sources such as the Qabalah, ancient Egypt, Pythagoras, ancient Greek Hermetics, and the Gnostics. The Eastern mystery traditions developed from spiritual philosophies such as Buddhism, Taoism, and Hinduism.

Ascended masters are guides who will often partner with a group that is focused on spiritual evolution—meditation groups, members of magickal lodges or Spiritualist churches, for example. They typically work with a collective group of souls to further the evolution of the planet as a whole, rather than just communicating with one or a few individuals. They will often also oversee and give guidance, energy, and wisdom to energy healers like Reiki masters and chakra balancers. An ascended master who appears as a spirit guide is a being who once led a physical life and has moved on to a higher spiritual plane, like a bodhisattva in Buddhist tradition. Examples of possible ascended masters include Buddha, the bodhisattva Kwan Yin, a Catholic saint, Krishna, or Mary Magdalene. Although the ascended master was once in a physical human form, throughout their last lifetime they actively sought to blend and balance spirit with their physical life. Upon death, they have chosen to remain close to human life in order to act as a link to spirit and serve as a mentor, protector, and teacher to all humankind. While ascended masters are concerned with the big picture, they are different than light beings. Light beings have never experienced life in a physical form—they have always been beings consisting solely of energy, not physical matter—and they do not always understand the limitations that human physical form and emotional response can present. Ascended masters *have* been in physical form, usually many times, as they have worked within many lifetimes in the physical world, perfecting their souls and their intentions.

If you have an ascended master assisting you, you are one of many souls that he or she is helping. Many times an ascended master will also have access to the akashic records. The akashic records (*akasha* is a Sanskrit word meaning "sky," "space," or "ether") is a term used in theosophy and anthroposophy to describe a collection of knowledge regarding both individual souls and the oversoul of a group, nation, or community that is contained in a nonphysical plane of existence. This akashic plane or level has existed since creation and contains the records of the spiritual evolution of the universe. Ascended masters are also sometimes referred to as master teacher guides.

If you find that you are drawn to a particular time in history and a specific geographical location, start investigating the possibilities for contact with an ascended master who was originally associated with that time and place. Are you fascinated with Egypt? Begin to study the Egyptian dynasties; learn about the gods and goddesses of Egypt; read accounts of historical Egyptian priests and priestesses, scribes, rulers, and healers; decorate the place where you meditate with Egyptian art and statuary; wear a piece of jewelry in the ancient Egyptian style. Begin to immerse yourself in the energy of your chosen time and place.

Perhaps you are attracted to Zen Buddhism or are interested in the philosophy of Taoism. Read about the precepts; learn who's who in those traditions; decorate your meditation space with symbols, fabrics, and art from that culture. When you meditate, use one of the major symbols from that path to explore in your focus.

Next you will be ready to open yourself to potential contact with an ascended master of that spiritual lineage. Begin by grounding and centering yourself. With focused breathing, fill your meditation space with the light exercise outlined in Exercise 15 on page 65.

Recite a short prayer, such as:

Protected and sustained by the Light,
I open myself to receiving Wisdom.
I will use this Guidance for the highest good
For myself and all living.

Next, state out loud or in your mind the name of the ascended master with whom you are seeking contact. Invite them to speak with you or show you a sign or omen that they are willing to work with you. You may feel a sudden breeze in the air, a book might fall off a shelf, you may hear the singing of a bird. These are signs of a presence and will be a signal to you in the future when contact is being made.

Remain quiet and centered to allow the communication to occur. You may receive immediate contact, or it may take several meditations to open the dialogue. Be sure to stay consciously aware that you are seeking the connection so that you pay attention to information you may receive outside of the meditation. You may receive information in your dreams, or as you go about your regular day by subtle things you encounter (a billboard that you pass that gives you a flash of information, for example, or a conversation that you overhear while waiting in line at the bank), or in omens and signs you receive over time. These signs can be subtle, such as seeing a robin or a ladybug in the dead of winter, a cloud formation that is in the distinct shape of a chalice, a rainbow prism of light that flashes before you. But when you receive this type of sign or omen, you will also receive a knowing, a clairaudient message or a sudden vision, which will bring you to immediate attention of the contact and the information that is being offered.

Teacher or Mentor Guides

The teacher or mentor is another form that a guide may take. The way we experience this form of guide is usually in a way that is symbolic or archetypal. In other words, the way that the guide presents themselves to you is in a human form, which is familiar to you from stories, myths, and legends. Many times in meditations, during which we are seeking wisdom and guidance, we encounter a guide in the human form of a sage, an old wise woman, or a storyteller at a campfire. We may meet a wry, old Asian monk or a lovely fairy-like child who takes our hand and leads us into an ancient forest during a meditation.

In the meditation (or in a dream) we tend to see this guide in a form and with trappings that we associate with wisdom and comfort. Teacher or mentor guides often appear when we are working on a specific problem. In this case, they have appeared to you for a specific purpose—to help you solve a current problem. This type of guide will appear in order to teach you a specific lesson, and to help you in a specific circumstance, and then go on to help someone else when your problem is solved.

Teacher or mentor guides may introduce you to other guides as well—guides who can help you problem-solve another situation and respond to your needs for guidance. These types of guides are encountered most easily during meditation or in your dreams while you are dealing with a special event. Once the situation is balanced or resolved, a teacher or mentor guide will consider the problem taken care of, and will then move on to help someone else. You can make this kind of contact by meditating on a particular problem that you are having and consciously asking for guidance and help to solve the problem.

EXERCISE 18: CONTACTING A TEACHER GUIDE

Prepare yourself in the usual way with your meditative breath and light exercise at a time and in a place where you will not be interrupted or distracted.

As you complete your light meditation exercise you will continue in the active meditation by creating the astral or energy place for connecting with and conversing with your teacher guide. In your mind's eye, you will begin to visualize a place to meet and talk with your guide. This place could be the seashore, a clearing in a forest, a beautiful garden filled with flowers, a mountaintop, an ancient temple . . . anywhere. As the images come to you, begin to infuse them with your energy. Deepen the colors, bring detail to the image, and add scent, sound, and sensation. It is as if you are building a place, and you are using energy imagery from your mind and psychic senses. You will use the same imagery of this place each time you begin this work to contact your teacher guide, so that it becomes familiar to you, and so that the instant you visualize this place you begin to make contact. Ask your guide to join you here; this act allows you to be in control.

You will find that this visualization method creates the initial contact with the guide. A link initiated from the teacher guide to you will be easy and instantaneous to recognize when it occurs. You will experience a sign from your astral meeting place: the scent of the place, a sound you associate with the place, a sudden vision of the place, and know that you need to open and pay attention for the information that the teacher guide has for you.

While a teacher or mentor guide can bring to your attention something that you should be working on in your spiritual growth, you will find that the guidance and wisdom you receive from them will be of the most help when you are intentionally working toward a spiritual goal, and are seeking the next step in your development. If ever you feel as if you have reached a dead end in your work, or you are not sure what the next step should be, this is the most valuable time to dialogue with your teacher guide.

Angelic Guides

Angelic guides are yet another form of guide. They are particularly prevalent in the Western world, with its rich history of Jewish, Christian, and Islamic religious traditions. Guides will come to people in the form that the individual will respond to most openly. For people who follow Western spiritual paths, guides can appear in the form of angels. Some people call an angel guide their guardian angel. The word angel comes from the Greek *angelos*, meaning "messenger," "envoy," or "announcer." In Hebrew, the name for angel is *mal'ach*, meaning "messenger." Angels are benevolent celestial energy beings who act as intermediaries or messengers between Divine Spirit, the heavens, the universe, and the earth and physical beings (plants, animals, humans) that populate the earth. They also interact with the elements of the earth—water, air, fire, soil—in an effort to keep all things balanced.

The concepts of angelic communication, protection, and intervention are ancient, and have been noted widely within the liturgy of Christianity, Judaism, and Islam. In these spiritual practices, angels are an important source of wisdom, guidance, and comfort.

Angels tend to be depicted in Western art as the image of a human figure with a halo and wings, but this image is a human representation of the angelic energy form for the convenience of the human mind. When interacting with an angel, you may see him or her in this traditional humanized Western form. (Although seeing an angel as a he or she is a human construct, too. Angels do not really have a gender identity.) But, there are several other ways that the angelic presence can be presented to you as you experience angelic contact. You may perceive a vision of coalescing, swirling light, which is a visual manifestation of the energy of their form. You may see either a simple human figure or one with wings and a halo. You may also see a radiating orb of light suspended in the air. The form that the angel takes will depend on what the angelic presence thinks you will respond to most easily—the form it believes you will be able to relate to best.

People experience this angelic presence as a guardian spirit or a guiding influence. Like any other guide, they cannot compel you to do anything. They will give you advice, healing, signs to convey their presence, protection, and direction, but as with all guides, you always use your own free will when you decide whether to utilize their guidance or not.

THE ANGELIC HIERARCHY

In Western religion and philosophy, there is what is called the angelic hierarchy. This is a system codifying all forms that angels may take and defining the different types of angels and levels of angelic service. Each level, or order, is in charge of specific duties and responsibilities to keep the balance and the function of that level of energy at its highest and most harmonious.

At the top of the angelic hierarchy, the orders are the Seraphim, Cherubim, and Thrones. The next level contains the Dominions, Virtues, and Powers. Last are the Principalities, Archangels, and Messenger Angels.

The Seraphim, Cherubim, and Thrones serve as counselors. These orders disperse information and commands directly from the Divine Source to the other lower levels of angelic beings to carry out. The Seraphim exert their influence for humanitarian or planetary causes. They surround the throne of the Divine and issue directives from the Divine to the ranks of angels as they do their work. The Seraphim are beings of pure light energy, and in addition to directing the Divine's influence toward humanitarian and planetary causes, they also work to keep the energy emanating from the physical world, directed toward Divinity, pure and positive in nature. As the Seraphim are so close to the Divine Source, they do not have individual names.

The Cherubim are the angels of harmony and wisdom. They are the guardians of light and of the stars. They provide guidance, divine protection, knowledge, and wisdom. The Cherubim direct energy to the Divine. Like the Seraphim, they do not have individual names.

The Thrones are often described as tiny iridescent spheres, circles, or wheels of energy and light. They move back and forth within another wheel or circle of energy that moves sideways and is set with numerous eyes. The Thrones are the wheels seen by Ezekiel and John in the Book of Revelation. Their main concerns in terms of balance on the earth are political, military, and economic in nature. The Thrones collect and disperse incoming and outgoing energy from the Divine. They are connected with the planets, as well as the four fixed constellations of the zodiac: Aquarius, Leo, Taurus, and Scorpio. The Thrones act on planetary issues, dispensing justice and Divine will.

Next are the Dominions, Virtues, and Powers, who act as governors, determining and governing how the directives from the level of Seraphim, Cherubim, and Thrones can best be carried out and accomplished by the Principalities, Archangels, and Messenger Angels.

The Dominions are angels of leadership and wisdom. They oversee the duties of the lower angels and keep the cosmos in order. They serve as divine leaders helping to balance and unify the spiritual world with the material world. The Dominions oversee order in the Law of Cause and Effect and make adjustments when the highest humanistic interests are not followed by churches, politicians, and other human leaders. They provide guidance for mediation, arbitration, and wise choices. In human perception of their presence and energies, the Dominions resemble a psychedelic mist or haze and are the bearers of conscience and the keepers of history. They are the angels of birth and death, sometimes accompanying a soul to or from a physical body. Their duties are also concerned with inspiring deep philosophy and theology as well as the distribution of power among mankind.

The Virtues are angels of movement and choice—they move Divine energy to the earth plane and work to elevate human consciousness so that humans are acting from free choice in balance with true and free will. They are sometimes known as "The Miracle Angels"—intervening in life-threatening situations. When sending spiritual energy to the collective human consciousness, they particularly help those individuals and organizations that work to alleviate suffering in the world and make it a better place. The Virtues bless and assist loving, positive people who are working to help, enlighten, and lead others toward harmony. As angels of the elements Earth, Air, Fire, and Water, the Virtues also oversee planetary upheaval, weather patterns, and the health of both the planet and of human individuals and communities. They are also thought to be the sparks of light that inspire mankind in the arts and sciences.

The Powers are angels of space and form. Their duties are to keep track of human history, aid religious leaders to serve the people (not their own egos), and dispense justice for individuals. The Powers send messages via Messenger Angels to an individual if harm is coming toward them. They disperse their energy and intervention for protection, defense, and the resolution of difficult situations involving the home, family, and friends.

Seraphim, Cherubim, Thrones, Dominions, Virtues, and Powers do not interact directly with humans. They oversee the larger workings and spiritual unfolding of our planet and our universe. Their guidance and directives are carried out on our physical level by the Principalities, Archangels, and Messenger Angels, who are the angelic worker bees, as they interact directly with humans and the physical realm.

The Principalities are angels of time and personality. The Principalities are said to resemble light rays. They are the guardian angels of the world's nations, and the political, military, and economic issues of these nations are the Principalities' main concern, including deciding who among humanity will be leaders and rulers. Their duties are to guard and balance continents, countries, cities, and large groups of people such as ecological organizations. The Principalities work toward global reform, channeling positive energy from the Divine. They are protectors of politics, governments, and religion. Their guidance is focused on how to solve the extinction of animals, leadership problems, human rights, and discrimination against minority groups.

ARCHANGELS

The word archangel is a compound word composed of the Greek words *arch* meaning "higher" or "original" and *angelos* meaning "messenger," "high messenger," or "original messenger." Archangels extend their energies toward endeavors of great importance to mankind's evolution and act as administrators to the other heavenly beings.

Archangels are also known as ruling angels, and are able to belong to and act within several levels in the angelic hierarchy. They enjoy human contact, and there are many references to them in world history, lore, and anecdote. The Archangels are the heads of the Angelic Hosts. They stand midway between the primal, archetypal level of force represented by the Seraphim, Cherubim, Thrones, Dominions, Virtues, and Powers and the building, actively working level of the Principalities and the Messenger Angels who interact directly with the physical world and intercede on its behalf.

Each Archangel can be contacted directly by name through meditation, ceremony, or prayer. In the mystery teachings of the Qabalah, each Archangel has the following name, powers, and responsibilities, as well as a position on the Tree of Life:

✧ Metatron is the Archangel of Kether, whose name translates as "near Thy throne," or the source of all things in the universe. Metatron filters the pure energy of the Divine Source into a vibration, which can be used and experienced in physical form without destroying the physical form. One might view Metatron's work like an electrical transformer, taking the high voltage energy from an electric plant down to a voltage that we humans can use as electrical power in our homes.

✧ Ratziel is the Archangel of Chokmah, whose name translates as "messenger or envoy of the Divine." Ratziel reveals Divinity as it emanates Divine energy into everything, and allows human consciousness to expand to the degree that it is able to comprehend the existence of Divinity.

⋄ Tzaphkiel is the Archangel of Binah, whose name translates as "beholder of the Divine." Tzaphkiel aids contemplation, meditation, and trance work to enable the seeker to understand Divinity on an intuitive level.

⋄ Auriel is the Archangel of Da'ath, whose name translates as "fire of the Divine." Auriel facilitates change and transformation, and puts the individual into contact with true will.

⋄ Tzadkiel is the Archangel of Chesed, whose name translates as "scribe of the Divine." Tzadkiel brings the order that exists in Divine laws into physical manifestation and expression on the earth and other planets.

⋄ Khamael is the Archangel of Geburah, whose name translates as "the seer of the Divine." Khamael brings Divine order and justice into physical being in such a way that purification occurs, and balance is achieved. Khamael brings light to injustice and destroys what is out of balance or no longer useful or needed so that new life and new ways can take root and grow.

⋄ Michael is the Archangel of Tiphareth, whose name translates as "who is as the Divine." Michael protects the soul of the individual and the planet. He helps bring the individual to inner balance so that the individual can express his or her own innate divinity.

⋄ Haniel is the Archangel of Netzach, whose name translates as "grace of the Divine." Haniel aids the individual in knowing Divinity through the physical senses, and expressing love purely.

Haniel also works to keep the ecological balance of the earth so that this planet is fertile and full of creative force.

✧ Raphael is the Archangel of Hod, whose name translates as "healer of the Divine." Raphael maintains the balance of the atmosphere of the planet and oversees the healing of the earth and her inhabitants. Raphael is also involved in teaching the inner mysteries and translating them into conscious thought.

✧ Gabriel is the Archangel of Yesod, whose name translates as "power of the Divine." Gabriel maintains the purity of the planet's water, and the fertility of humans, plant life, and animals. He acts as a direct messenger of the Divine through the vehicle of dreams.

✧ Sandalphon is the Archangel of Malkuth, whose name translates as "wearer of sandals," meaning the one who leads the aspirant in his or her soulful journey back to the Divine Source. Sandalphon organizes energy so that it can manifest in balance in physical form. Sandalphon is also the direct protector of the planet Earth.

MESSENGER ANGELS

Messenger Angels are the ones most familiar to humankind. The main concerns of Messenger Angels are those day-to-day concerns of basic human affairs and activities, and they work to protect and guide individual humans. They also act as messengers and envoys between heaven and the earth.

These Messenger Angels are the symbolic builders of the universe, the construction workers who serve the One Divine Architect under the direction of "foremen," the Archangels. Each Messenger

Angel has specific duties and responsibilities as assigned to them by the Archangels and Principalities. These angels are a part of what are called the Angelic Hosts.

These types of angels have thousands of various individual names, but are collectively known as Messenger Angels, Nature Angels, and Guardian Angels. An individual angel can be assigned or connected to a human as a personal or family guardian angel, and is involved in human development, human evolution, and physical manifestation as pertains to an individual person. Messenger Angels help to channel energy from the Divine to a human at an energy frequency level and in a form that can be comfortably used by the person.

Typically, an angel needs to be asked for help. Only in an emergency will an angel interfere with a human's free will, and that interference will only come if the human has not yet completed the sacred contract that they set out in this lifetime to achieve. The angel's interference will be to attempt to give guidance to help the person make the best choice or take the best action to further the development of their soul. But, as always, the person has free will as to the choice he or she makes or the action that is taken—the angel cannot compel behavior within that individual. Messenger Angels guide in times of life transformation such as death or birth. They serve in defense and protection of an individual person and can be asked directly for advice or guidance. But you, the human, are free to take the guidance or not.

How do you make direct contact with an angel in a conscious fashion? Contact is made through meditation, prayer, ceremony, or, in some circumstances, by simply asking. Whenever you choose to make contact with angelic forces, you should begin by relaxing into an alpha state consciousness. You may choose to seek your help from a specific angelic presence, or leave all contact options open.

EXERCISE 19: CONNECTING WITH ANGELIC ENERGY THROUGH MEDITATION OR PRAYER

You will begin by sitting or standing quietly, slowing your breathing, and focusing your energies by grounding them with those of the earth and the heavens above.

Once you are grounded and centered within yourself, you can begin your meditation. As you focus your mind on the problem for which you are asking help, allow your consciousness to drift slightly. Open your awareness and receptivity as you meditate. If there is a particular angel you believe will be the most helpful, you may address them by name. Simply repeat the angelic name in your mind or out loud in a slow rhythm, leaving ten seconds or so between repetitions until you feel their presence. If you don't know the name of a particular angel, focus on your intention of finding help for your problem and leave it up to the angelic energy presences around you to know which one can best offer you guidance toward a solution. You may hear an answer within your mind or just outside your ears, you may have a vision that contains a symbol or a sign that gives you the answer, or you may receive a sudden knowing of the answer. There is also the possibility that you may not receive an answer at that precise moment, but you may receive the information you need in your dreams or by an omen over the next few days.

If you choose prayer as your vehicle of communication and ask for guidance during the prayer, you will again start by creating a calm, serene mindset. Keep your prayer short, direct, and

continued on the next page

continued from the previous page

simple. Address your angel by name if you know it. If you have not made previous contact, simply ask that an angelic being work with you and on your behalf in regard to the problem. Again, you may receive immediate information, guidance, or directive during or just following your prayer. Or, help may come to you in a sign, in a dream, or in a sudden unexpected solution over the next few days.

EXERCISE 20: CONNECTING WITH ANGELIC ENERGY THROUGH RITUAL

You may receive the best angelic help by using this ritual. Begin by setting up an altar, upon which you will place one or more candles as an offering of light, and any pictures or objects that you associate with angelic energies (crystals, fresh flowers, a bell, or something of that nature). If you will be working with a specific angel, you may want to also use an altar cover in a color associated with that angel's energy and perhaps any symbols associated with the angel as well. If you are new to angelic workings, you will want to do a bit of research into the symbols and colors that would be appropriate. Next create a sacred energy space within the room you will be working.

Using your meditative breathing and light visualization, ground, center, and open yourself and your psychic senses. Light the candles on your altar as you begin to initiate this angelic energy contact and state simply and clearly the help or advice that you are seeking. Then sit or lie quietly as you maintain your focus by gazing at the candle flames and await your answer. Again, you may receive immediate information, guidance, or directive during or just following your ritual, or help may come over the next few days.

Of course, sometimes we encounter a situation in which we just simply need to ask for help and there is not time for meditation or ritual. If your need is great and your emotions high, simply stating out loud what you need can work. It's better if you can create a calm state of mind and get yourself grounded, centered, and open before you begin, but that is not always possible when you are facing a sudden danger or crisis. In the case of an emergency, state your need out loud and open yourself to the guidance and help that will be offered to you.

The guidance and help from the angelic realm is a two-way street. All acts of energy exchange should be reciprocal to maintain balance. After you have made your angelic request, immediately give thanks and perform an act of kindness or charity as your reciprocal payment for that help. You may light a novena candle as you state your thanks or radiate the energy of appreciation. You may show your thanks by taking your invalid neighbor's dog for a walk. You may choose to smile at strangers you meet with the conscious knowledge that you are doing this to bring a little light and positive connection into the world. You may choose to plant something or volunteer at a phone help line as your way of thanks. Whatever you do to reciprocate, acknowledge why you are doing it: to express appreciation and give thanks for what you have received or are expecting to receive.

You may wish to initiate an angelic connection to create a relationship with the angelic realm, so that when you need help, you already have an established contact. If this is the case, you may use any of the examples above—meditation, prayer, ceremony, or simply asking—to begin the conversation with an angelic guide. Plan to make time at least once a week for your angelic meditation, prayer, ceremony, or supplication. As you begin to make and strengthen this angelic connection and dialogue, you will find that in the future, when you ask for it, you will receive advice, help, and guidance very quickly and directly, even when you are facing an emergency and need intervention immediately.

With any experiences with any type of guide, don't expect some disembodied voice to suddenly start speaking loudly into your ear. You may hear information, but generally it is heard within the mind, or feels like it is being spoken to you somewhere around your head, usually toward the ear that is on the same side of your body as your dominant hand—the hand you write with. Spirit guides will speak to you in your thoughts, sometimes using words, but also using images, symbols, and feelings. You will experience more of a subtle knowing, and your understanding will come from feeling the answers as they come to you, as well as analyzing the spoken information. Remember, do not try to force the information. Let it come to you. If you try to force the experience, you will engage your conscious mind, not your subconscious mind, and that subconscious mind is the part of yourself you are seeking to develop. When you get a message from spirit, it doesn't generally come in the form of a cryptic symbol or image that you don't comprehend. You don't usually need to interpret your clairvoyant images like you do your dreams. When there's something you need to know spiritually, it is usually given to you in the easiest, simplest way that helps you to understand what you need to do to create the future you are working toward.

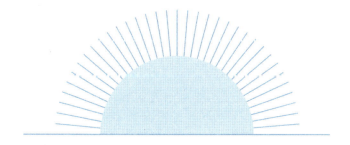

CHAPTER 5

Psychic Dreaming

A dream is defined as "a series of images, ideas, emotions, and sensations occurring involuntarily in the mind during certain stages of sleep." The experience of dreaming is common to both humans and animals. We all have several dream scenarios each night, whether we remember them or not. We have all witnessed our pets dreaming, as they bark or scramble their feet in a semblance of running as they lie asleep in the corner. Not all dreams have important messages to impart to us—many times dreams simply allow us to sleep in a deep and completely relaxed physical state, while being entertained, in a sense, by the stories that unfold within our minds as we rest. But dreams can also be the language of the soul and the subconscious mind. The images, dream inhabitants, experiences, and story lines of our dreams can reveal our concerns, aspirations, fears, and hopes.

A dream tends to include images, thoughts, scenarios, and emotions that are all experienced simultaneously during a person's sleep cycle. They are sometimes amazingly focused and vivid; other times they are vague, unclear, and confusing with conflicting and baffling imagery or experiences. Our dreams can be filled with emotions of happiness or fear, enjoyment or dread, and we feel those emotions intensely, without censure, during the dream. Dreams indicate what is happening in our psyches and bring to light issues, inspirations, and knowledge that reside in our subconscious and deeper unconscious minds. In telling these stories, they often speak to us using the language of symbols. It is then our job to interpret those symbols and the emotions that they evoke during the dream in order to understand the meaning behind, and the value of, the dream information we have received.

Dream interpretation is the process of assigning meaning to the events, symbols, images, feelings, and people that we experience in our dream states. In many ancient societies, dreaming was considered a supernatural communication or a means of divine intervention—an important message from the gods or from spirits that needed to be seriously listened to. This message would be unraveled by the temple priesthood, who were gifted in the interpretation of dream symbolism and the emotional response of the dreamer to those symbols. In Greece and Egypt, there were "sleep" or "incubation" temples dedicated to Asclepius, the god of healing and medicine. These temples were used by the populace as a sacred place to receive physical and mental healing, using their dreams as a guide to understanding the basis of their ailment. Through practices of chanting, fasting, meditation, and ritual bathing, the patients would be prepared for the dream experience and led into a trancelike state by the priests of the temple. The patient would move from the trance into the sacred, healing sleep state and report the events, images, and feelings they experienced upon awakening. This dream information was used to determine what the foundation of the illness or imbalance was, and to help the priest or physician decide upon the best type of treatment for the individual.

Learning to remember and interpret your dreams can help you discover the hidden messages that you receive as you sleep, giving you insight and guidance into what is happening within you and your soul at deeper levels. Remembering your dreams and interpreting their events and symbols will help you comprehend the psychic nudges you are privy to in your sleep, and give you information about things within yourself that you may want to change or pay particular attention to as you work to make events in your life better or to enhance the opportunities that are waiting at your doorstep.

Over the last century or so, various schools of psychology have offered differing theories about the meaning of dreams and why we dream in the first place. One theory is that dreams are simply a relaxing product of sleep and have no intrinsic deeper meaning or use. Another theory is that through the experience of dreaming, a person lets go of the concerns of their day-to-day lives, allowing them to refresh their mental and emotional perspectives while resting the body. The theory that dreams help to reveal the inner workings of a person and their psyche was brought to public attention with the 1899 publication in Germany of Sigmund Freud's arguably most famous and influential book, *The Interpretation of Dreams*. It was with this published work that the modern Western world regained its interest in the meaning and value of dreams. In his book, Freud postulated that dreams were an important tool in understanding the underlying psychological health and motivations, both conscious and unconscious, of an individual. He wrote about his own dreams as well as several clinical case studies of patients with whom he was working and explained why he believed the activity within their dreams had an important bearing in their inner psychological worlds. Freud writes in the introduction of *The Interpretation of Dreams*:

> In the following pages, I shall demonstrate that there exists a psychological technique by which dreams may be interpreted and that upon the application of this method every dream will show itself to be a senseful psychological structure which may be introduced into

an assignable place in the psychic activity of the waking state. I shall furthermore endeavor to explain the processes which give rise to the strangeness and obscurity of the dream, and to discover through them the psychic forces, which operate whether in combination or opposition, to produce the dream.

In this passage, Freud was using the term "psychic" in the sense of the inner motivating soul, not psychic work as we are discussing it in the pages of this work. As part of his theory of understanding and interpreting dreams, he described two different classifying components of dreams: their manifest content, made up of images, story lines, thoughts, and emotions; and the latent content, which is the interpretation of the experiences and energies present in the dream (those components which represent the underlying and perhaps hidden psychological meaning of the dream). His work captured the interest and imagination of the professional world of psychiatry, as well as the public at large, and became a core resource used then and today in psychological therapy.

While some modern research suggests that our dreams don't serve any real purpose, considering the amount of time we spend dreaming, it only makes sense that dreaming is important to our physical, emotional, mental, and spiritual well-being. And, certainly, ancient sources have always contended that dreams are an important source for communing with and obtaining psychic wisdom from the Divine, as a source of prophecy, and in understanding the state of a human being and their psyche. In ancient Greece, the interpretation of dreams was part of the diagnosis of the underlying foundation of an illness by physicians. The father of modern Western medicine, Hippocrates, regularly used his interpretations of his patient's dreams to help direct him in their treatment.

By interpreting your dreams, you can gain a deep understanding about what your subconscious mind is bringing to the attention of your conscious, everyday mind. This understanding will help you work out problems, solve situations, gain creative insight, and tap into your own intuition. All of the symbols, people, places, or events that you experience while in a dream state create some kind of reaction in you. As you interpret your dreams, pay particular attention to the symbols that get the strongest emotional reaction in you— they are the keys to the meaning of the dream. But it is not only the interpretation of your dreams that brings value to working psychically with dream-produced information. There are many ways to purposefully and intentionally use your dreams to obtain knowledge about future events, to make deliberate changes within your subconscious mind for more success in your life, to transform blocks such as fear or lack of confidence into strengths, to open your psychic skills and awareness to greater depth and accuracy, to make contact with spirit guides and your higher self, and much more.

The information that we can access in our dreams is provided by our subconscious in a very efficient way, often addressing multiple issues on multiple topics all in one dream story line. A single dream can warn you of health dangers, predict the future, point out personality flaws (or credits), and present a solution to a current problem. Some dreams that you experience are worthy of repeated analysis. Just because you can come up with two or three interpretations, that does not mean that only one interpretation can be right. In fact, they could all easily be right as you apply your analysis and intuition to all of the issues the dream may be illuminating.

Scientists have been studying dreams intently for the last century and a half, postulating differing theories about the value and purpose of dreaming. They have sought to explain why we dream and what the purpose of dreams may be. We spend one third of our lives in sleep, but we have not reached a consensus about why we dream. Today's scientists have discovered how to record the brain wave energy patterns of people during their sleep cycles using EEG (electroencephalography) machines. The brain's electrical wave pattern frequencies reveal that there are five different brain wave stages that occur during the process of sleep, each correlating to a specific state of being in the individual. While moving into the earliest phase of sleep, stage one, a person is still relatively awake and alert. The brain still produces beta waves—the same wave frequency which is associated with waking consciousness. As the processes of the brain begin to slow down and relax, the beta brain waves slow to an alpha brain frequency in a process that generally takes fifteen to twenty minutes. This is the transition from the waking brain state into the state of sleep, the beginning of the sleep cycle, and it is a light stage of semi-consciousness. It is during this time that people sometimes experience what feel like unusual, vivid sensations such as the feeling of suddenly falling. These are known as hypnagogic hallucinations.

The alpha brain wave state then deepens into the very slow frequency theta brain wave state, which is the transition into stage two of the sleep cycle. At this point, the brain begins to produce rapid bursts of rhythmic activity, although the body's temperature begins to decrease and the heart rate slows. Next, the deepest brain wave state begins to occur with stage three sleep, as we transition into the delta state, with its slowest brain wave frequency. This transition into the delta brain wave brings us into the stage four state, and we are in a full delta brain wave pattern, deeply unconscious and unaware of our surroundings.

The last part of the sleep cycle is stage five, and this is where we experience our dreams intensely. In this level of unconsciousness, we are in the state called REM (rapid eye movement) sleep which is characterized by eye movement under our eyelids, faster breathing, and increased brain activity. During this last cycle, the brain and our other organs, like the kidneys and liver, become more active, while our muscles become more relaxed. We begin to dream because of this increased brain activity, but our voluntary muscles have become almost paralyzed. Our brains are aware of the action within the dream, but we seldom physically move while in this deeply relaxed state, unless the events in our dream become such that our brains direct us into a fight-or-flight response, which abruptly brings us back to a state of consciousness, usually breathing very quickly, sometimes vocalizing, and with adrenaline flooding our body.

When we begin to develop the conscious ability to dream, we enable ourselves to use our dream states and their stories in a purposeful fashion: to foretell the future with precognitive dreaming; to gain access to the wisdom of a spirit guide or loved one who is deceased; to discover our past lives; to stimulate the memory to retrieve information we have been trying to recall in our waking life; to send telepathic dreams to others; to receive answers from our higher selves for solving problems; to have dialogue with our subconscious mind to encourage creativity and awaken our psychic talents; and to receive psychic messages from omens, our guides, and the Divine.

Throughout history, people have had precognitive dreams that have revealed events to come. Perhaps one of the most famous examples is in the Book of Genesis, in the story about Joseph, son of Jacob and Rachel. Born in Canaan, he was known to his family to have a talent for precognitive dreams and their interpretation. Sold into slavery by his brothers, he arrived in Egypt to serve Potiphar, the captain of Pharaoh's guard. He served as supervisor of the household until he was falsely accused by Potiphar's wife of trying to rape her. He was thrown into prison and remained there for several years. During his time in prison, several of his prophetic dreams became known for their accuracy. One night, Pharaoh had a pair of dreams which awakened him in a panic. He felt great dread about the dreams he had experienced and was desperate to understand what they meant. One of his dreams featured seven lean cows that rose out of the waters of the Nile to devour seven fat cows. The other dream was of seven withered, rotting shafts of grain which devoured seven fat, succulent shafts. None of Pharaoh's advisors had been able to interpret these dreams for him, but one of Pharaoh's servants remembered hearing about Joseph and spoke of his skill in dreaming and dream interpretation to Pharaoh. Joseph was summoned before the court and interpreted the dreams as foretelling that there would be seven years of great abundance which would be followed by seven years of devastating famine. He advised Pharaoh to store surplus grain during the years of abundance, and Pharaoh did. Indeed, these events took place as Joseph had interpreted, and, in his gratitude, Pharaoh appointed Joseph Vizier of Egypt, with responsibilities to help rule Egypt.

In precognitive dreaming, the images, the story, and the emotions within the dream are all important to its clear interpretation. Like the story above, many precognitive dreams give their information in symbology, not as a direct blow-by-blow telling of events exactly as they will transpire in the physical world. Sometimes dream dictionaries may be initially helpful in interpreting images and events in a dream, but ultimately you will find their help to be limited. There are some symbols that are considered archetypal—meaning that they tend to be interpreted the same way in all cultures. Dreaming of a mother as a symbol, for example, would signify nurturance, love, caretaking, and life giving in every culture. The sun tends to be a symbol of life, health, and success universally. But not all symbols are universal. In fact, most aren't. When you are working to interpret images and events within a dream, you will need to decide if the symbol has a personal meaning for you or not before you pull out your dream dictionary. For example, in Western culture the dog tends to symbolize friendship, protection, and loyalty. But if you were attacked and frightened by a dog in your childhood, for you a dog might symbolize danger. Depending on how you react to dogs emotionally, that symbol in your dream could have different meanings. In the Muslim world, dogs are seen as dirty, lowly creatures, not family members as they are in the West. If you are a devout Muslim dreaming about a dog, the dog image would tend to symbolize disgrace or the lack of adherence to a religious law, not loyalty or friendship.

Keeping a dream journal is integral to successful psychic dreaming. Regardless of the type of dream experience or psychic dream goal you are working on, keeping a dream journal will help you to gain understanding of what the symbols you receive in a dream signify. You will begin to write your own personal dream dictionary by recording the images, scenes, animals, people, and events you experience in the dream state in your journal. Along with the recording of any types of images you receive, write down the feelings and emotions that accompany them. The feelings that you get will help you understand what each object, place, or person symbolizes. Leave plenty of space on each page of your journal to enable yourself to add more information, interpretation, and knowledge as your dream expertise grows with time and use. Later, when you are fleshing out the dream details, you may also wish to engage in the practice of automatic writing to allow your subconscious mind and your guides to provide additional insight. You can do this in the pages of the dream journal. Or, if you wish, you can transcribe your dreams into a document on your computer.

Precognitive dreaming can take place at a time when something important is about to happen and your subconscious mind picks up on the energy surrounding the event inadvertently without you purposefully seeking it out. You can also initiate receiving precognitive information via your dreams by determining exactly what future information you want. When you are working toward this goal, first you will decide what you wish to obtain knowledge about. Maybe you are curious about a future mate, the success or failure of an important project you are working on, or whether or not you will be offered the job you just interviewed for. Maybe you want to know the gender of a pregnant friend's baby.

When you are working to receive information within your dreams, you may find it more relaxing and easier if you sleep alone, particularly if you habitually sleep with a person or animal who is restless during the night. You will prepare by eating a very light dinner and abstaining from both caffeine and alcohol that day. Take care of all of your bedtime rituals prior to reclining so that your body will not need attention during your sleep cycles. Wear loose, comfortable clothing that will not twist around you or bind any part of your body. Unplug the phone and make sure that any animals in the household have their evening needs met before you retire as well. You may want to utilize a scent that helps to relax you while engaging your psychic senses by burning a small amount of incense, lighting a scented votive candle, or anointing your Third Eye with essential oil. Jasmine, sandalwood, wisteria, or neroli are all beautiful scents that work well for producing psychic results. Do not use any sleep aids such as sleeping pills—you want to keep your mind and your impressions as clear as possible for the process.

You may want to engage in some gentle stretching exercises or yoga asanas to help your body relax when you lie down.

EXERCISE 21: PREPARING FOR PSYCHIC DREAMING

When you are ready to retire, lie down and cover your body with just enough blankets so that your body will be a comfortable temperature for the night—you don't want to make yourself restless because you're too hot or too cold. Begin to relax your body and your mind, engaging in your meditative breath, slowing your breathing, exhaling any stress or tension. Allow the muscles of your body to feel as if they are slowly melting. (Sometimes I like to imagine that I am a rag doll filled with sand and I focus on all of the sand escaping from my hands and feet as I gently flatten out into complete relaxation.) Let your mind empty of everything except the question that you are seeking to answer in your dream. Repeat the question in your mind in a languid fashion, keeping a gentle focus. Just drift off to sleep naturally with the expectation that you will receive the answer you are opening to.

Have a journal or a recorder at the ready by the bed in a position that will make it easy to reach so that you can immediately note any images, feelings, and information you received at the moment that you begin to awaken. If you wake up in the middle of the night, note any impressions that you have gotten thus far and go back to sleep. Any time you awaken, note what images or feelings you have experienced in your dream. Don't try to make complete sentences, just write down or record the gist of what you are getting in single words or short phrases—you can fill it in later when you are in a fully conscious state and you don't want to bring yourself out of your alpha or delta brain state by engaging your conscious mind. In the morning, note anything else you have received in your dream state the

continued on the next page

continued from the previous page

night before and get ready to face your regular waking day. During the night, you may have gotten a very clear message or image that gives you your answer, or you may have gotten several pieces of the puzzle but not a definitive answer. If this is the case, work the next couple of nights with the same question and follow the same procedure of writing down what you are getting in your dreams any time that you awaken.

EXERCISE 22: SPIRIT GUIDE DREAMING

The dream state is very conducive to conversations with spirit guides of all types. You can utilize your dreams to make an initial psychic contact to develop a relationship with a guide, or to engage in dialogue with a guide with whom you already have contact. You will follow all of the steps as outlined above for precognitive dreaming, but for this type of guide dream work, your focus as you drift into sleep is on contacting a guide. If you do not already have a guide that you have an established working relationship with, your focus will be on making that connection. Your thoughts while going into the sleep state will be on opening to contact. You will state in your mind that you wish to contact a willing spiritual guide who has interest in your spiritual and psychic potential and growth for your higher good and the good of those around you. As you begin to make contact within your dream, you may see yourself in a temple, in an open airy glade, or within a warm, gentle mist. The contact may at first be via words or information you receive in your mind, but you may also see the form or image of the guide before you, seated or standing. The guide may appear to you in a human-like form, as a spirit animal, an orb of light, or any myriad of ways. During the first contact, don't worry about any specific questions beyond getting the name of the guide and what, in general, they wish to teach you.

As you work with your guide in your dreams in the future, you may have some specific questions about spiritual practices you are following, how to resolve a problem or conflict you are experiencing, what your next step should be in your spiritual development, or topics such as these. But for the first contact, just concentrate on what the guide's energy feels like to you, so that you can recognize it in future dreams or when working with that guide in other psychic ways.

Past-life dreaming can be fascinating and illuminating. Knowing what types of experiences your soul has had can give you understanding of what you have come into this lifetime to achieve. You can get information about the spiritual connections you have with some of the important people in your present life and comprehend why you have the kind of relationships you have with them this time around. Knowing about your different past lives can help you understand why you react or feel the way that you do about particular places or people and can give you insight into some of your attitudes and behavior in this life. You can also discover what type of karmic debts you are here to repay and then make conscious decisions and choices about how to go about balancing those karmic debts. Like precognitive dreams, past-life dreams can be presented to you without you working to link with that information, but you can also deliberately seek to reconnect with a past life in your dream state. This past life can be one that you are already aware of, but are seeking to understand more about. You can also set up the past-life dream experience to obtain information about a past life that has not yet been revealed to you.

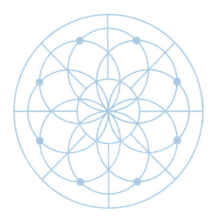

EXERCISE 23: PAST-LIFE DREAMING

For past-life dreaming, prepare yourself in the usual way. If you are wanting to discover additional information about a past life you already know a little bit about, as you begin to drift into sleep, picture in your mind's eye the way that you looked in that life, or a familiar landscape, dwelling, or place that you have seen before when you have reexperienced events in that past life. If you know your name during that lifetime, state it several times in your mind as you alter your conscious state of mind into the alpha wave brain state and relax your awareness into sleep. It may be the case in a past-life dream that you are simply looking to discover more information about that lifetime. If this is so, just allow the scenes and experiences of that life to unfold before you in your dream. If your purpose is to understand something specific regarding that lifetime, such as whether lessons you learned in that previous life are active gifts and abilities that you are using in this lifetime, or what karma you bring forward into this life from the past, have those specific questions at the front of your mind as you relax into sleep. As usual, be prepared to write or record any information you receive upon awakening.

EXERCISE 24: INFORMATION RETRIEVAL IN THE DREAM STATE

You can use your psychic dreaming skills to help you retrieve memories and information from your subconscious mind as well. As you float into the dream state, ask a specific question about whatever it is you are trying to recall. These can be mundane questions: Where did I put my passport? What is the name of my first grade teacher? What is the math equation that explains waves of sound energy? They can also be more serious questions: What are the underlying issues regarding the ongoing health problems I am having? Where should I be applying my energies right now? The memories and information that you are trying to uncover through this "fishing" in the subconscious mind to "hook" information does not only have to access memories contained in your mind. You know by now that we are creatures of energy living in a space composed of more levels and layers of energy that are interconnected and that act upon and within our own personal vibration and energy waves at all times. There is something that the renowned psychologist, Carl Jung, termed "the collective unconscious." In this level or realm of moving, fluidic energy source, all that has happened still resides, and all that has the potential to happen exists. You can fish this repository for information, experience, and wisdom in your dreams as well. Just determine the question, pose it to your subconscious in your dreams, and you can retrieve that knowledge as well. Some people called this collective unconscious repository of wisdom, experience, knowledge, and potential the akashic record.

Perhaps you'd like to experiment with sending telepathic messages in your dream state. Maybe there is an individual with whom you have lost contact over the years. As you go into your dream state, visualize them in your mind and state their name. Form a friendly message or greeting as you go into sleep and see it winging its way through time and space to your friend. Maybe you have had a conflict with someone you value and for some reason you cannot communicate with them through the usual channels of phone, letter, or email. Picture them in your mind's eye, state their name, and offer them a sincere apology and regret for your part of the disagreement as you move into your dream state. Then wait to see if they wish to respond to you in the waking state. They may not be receptive to further contact, and it is not ethical to continuously invade other people's dreams. If after the third try you do not receive acknowledgement or contact from them, drop it.

EXERCISE 26: RETRAINING THE MIND USING DREAMS

You can also use your psychic dreaming skills to awaken dialogue with your subconscious mind to strengthen and reinforce habits you wish to develop. It is possible to access your subconscious through your dreams to transform habits that you wish to stop or that are getting in your way. It is within the subconscious mind that habits, good or bad, reside. When any type of behavior becomes habitual, we act upon it without consciously thinking about it—the habitual behavior has become a part of our instinctual reaction to the world. Often the easiest and most straightforward way to transform a habit you no longer wish to have is to work directly on it via your dreaming subconscious mind.

Let's say that you are working on improving your follow-through and motivation. Pick two or three key words that really embody the concepts that make up your goal. After you have prepared yourself for a working dream session, as you drift into sleep, repeat these words like a meditation mantra to yourself and direct your subconscious mind to show you a dream where you are engaging in the behavior you are working to instill within yourself. Repeat this process several times a week during a month's time.

This is a form of lucid dreaming. Lucid dreaming is the process of being asleep and yet while in the dream state, completely conscious of the content and experience of the dream, as you choose to act or not act within the dream. Lucid dreaming can be used to make deliberate changes in your psyche and waking behavior.

If you are trying to transform a bad habit or rid yourself of habitual behavior, as you move into sleep, feel within your mind for where in your brain that habit has lodged itself. Once you have determined the location of the energy of that bad habit, visualize a cleansing light shining upon the area. Let the light dissolve the energy of the habit and allow your breath to carry that energy out and away from your mind. Work with this visualization over a month's time, a couple of times a week. At the end of that month, return again to the area within your brain where you removed the bad habit, this time with the concept of the transformed habit, which you will mentally place in that location. For example, if the bad habit that you are working to transform or rid yourself of involves overeating, first locate where that habit is lodged in the synapses of your brain.

Next, using your visualization of light, dissolve that habit and then use your exhaled breath to carry that energy away. This will be one month's work. The next step will be to replace the bad habit with the new behavior that you wish to exhibit, which for the purposes of this example will be replacing the habit of overeating with the new habit of exercise.

The second part of this dream working then will be to visualize yourself enjoying a brisk walk, a yoga workout, or performing a set of sit-ups. See yourself enjoying this behavior and implant that image in your mind as you are drifting into sleep. You will find that in your waking life, you will feel drawn to this activity, and will get a sense of enjoyment and fulfillment from it each time that you engage in it.

You can also work within your dream state to reinforce your development of your psychic skills. As you relax into your

continued on the next page

continued from the previous page

sleep, visualize your mind opening. Pay particular attention to the area of your Third Eye and the location of your pineal gland. This is a gland located in the center of your brain between the left and right hemispheres. The pineal gland is shaped like a pinecone and is about the size of a piece of rice. Among the many functions it serves is that of regulating the sleeping and waking cycles through its secretion of the hormone melatonin. As you begin to drift into sleep, moving from the waking beta wave state into the alpha wave state, visualize the color purple and begin to breathe this color into your auric system. Let this color surround and be absorbed by your Third Eye and pineal gland, infusing them with psychic sensitivity and awareness.

EXERCISE 27: COMMUNICATING WITH THE SPIRIT WORLD THROUGH DREAMS

You can also utilize the openness of your subconscious during your dream state to make contact with loved ones who have passed away. You may wish to make this connection to get an answer to a question that only that loved one has the answer to; you may wish to check in with them to see how they are doing in the spirit world; you could link to them in a dream to let them know that whatever differences or difficulties the two of you had while they were living have been resolved or forgiven by you.

If you would like to make this type of contact, allow yourself to get into the proper relaxed and open subconscious mind state as usual. Ground yourself and have an object link that involves the person with whom you wish to have contact—their picture, a piece of jewelry, a letter, an article of clothing—this will help make the link stronger and easier to create. As you move deeper into the sleep state, see the person you wish to communicate with in your mind's eye, state their name aloud or within your mind, and hold the object link in your hands or place it just under your pillow. Usually when you use your dreams to contact someone you knew when they were living, you will see them as they were in their body when alive. While you are involved in this dream contact with your loved one, you may experience their dream presence in what feels like a physical way—in your dream you may sit down at a table with them, you might meet them in a park, they may appear at the door of your home, or they may simply

continued on the next page

continued from the previous page

suddenly be by your side. Occasionally you may not see them at all, and will only hear their voice as they answer your questions or dialogue with you. But either way that you make the connection, record the experience and the information you receive in your dream journal so that you will be able to reference it in the future as needed. You may also find that after you have made this dream connection with your deceased friend or family member, in the future when they have something important to impart to you they will use your dreams to do so. After you have made the initial contact, they will feel free to communicate with you on their own.

For any type of active psychic work with your dreams, you will want to set the proper stage by doing your best to ensure that you will have a quiet, uninterrupted period of time to commune with your inner psyche, hence the need to sleep in a place where you will not be brought out of your work by a restless sleep partner, a ringing phone, or the physical need to visit the restroom. You will want to schedule your night for psychic dreaming when you can sleep in if you like and not have to be awakened by an alarm clock. Although you will experience dreams all night long, many times it is the dreams you experience just before waking that contain the most information or the clearest psychic connection. You will want your period of returning to your conscious waking state after dreaming to be calm and contemplative, giving you a chance to examine and remember all of the dream information you obtained the night before. If the phone rings or the alarm goes off, you will be jolted into consciousness and the dream information will be lost for the time being.

You may even want to follow the example of the ancients and create your own dream temple or dream chamber in a special, separate room in your home for your spiritual and psychic dream use. This space would be in the quietest part of the house and easily temperature controlled. It would not be cluttered with lots of extraneous decorations and bric-a-brac, but would instead be almost austere in its function and look. You only need a small bed with enough covers to keep your body comfortable while you explore your subconscious via your dreams, a few candles, a small bedside table on which to place your dream journal or recorder, and curtains to keep out any light. Any type of decoration in the room should be appropriate to the work: a beautiful crystal cluster, a statue of a god or goddess associated with dreaming, sleep, and psychic inspiration, a picture or poster that is inspirational to you in nature. You may want your dream chamber to be equipped with an incense burner and an incense in a scent that is conducive to psychic work. If you want scent, but are sensitive to smoke, you may choose to use an aroma burner instead and utilize an essential oil or essential oil blend to enhance your work.

If you have found that you habitually forget your dreams or are not even sure that you do dream, you may want to begin taking the mineral zinc in a 100 milligram supplement to help you experience and remember dreams better. In addition to helping you remember your dreams, zinc is also good for the skin, helps in brain neural function, and quickens the healing of cuts and wounds.

CHAPTER 6

Accessing Your Past Lives

As a part of your psychic work, you will often find that discovering who you have been in your past lives is a valuable tool in the work you are doing in this lifetime. What you did in each life, the other people or events that you were connected with, and the gifts and the challenges you experienced in those lifetimes are brought forward to this present life. Knowledge of your previous lives can inform you about the important things you need to focus on to achieve this life's purpose. This information helps to illuminate your understanding of yourself and the needs of your soul, and gives you insight into how you express yourself this time around as well as why you have some of the values and reactions to your soul's work in your present life and body.

Three-quarters of the world believes in some form of reincarnation—it is only in the modern Western world that the idea of reincarnation seems novel or far-fetched. The word reincarnation comes from Latin and literally means "entering the flesh again" (*re* meaning "again" and *incarnation* meaning "the flesh"). Depending on the spiritual teachings of each religious system, this reincarnation may be into human form or animal form, each type of body serving as a vehicle to house the soul as it develops, expands, evolves, and seeks to connect with the innate divinity that is the source of all.

Early Buddhist texts contain writings that discuss techniques involving deep meditation and prayer for the purpose of recalling previous lifetimes and their lessons. In Tibetan Buddhism particularly there is much importance and tradition surrounding reincarnation, its purpose, and how to go about remembering past lives and the important events within those lives. The well-known treatise *The Tibetan Book of the Dead* addresses how to die properly, how to transfer one's spiritual essence and intelligence into a new body, and how to locate the new physical vehicle which is now inhabited by the old soul. In Tibetan tradition, the reincarnation of a priest or *tulku* can take generations—it is not an instantaneous process. Between lives, while in the realm of spirit, there may be additional lessons or knowledge that needs to be learned, knowledge that will be applicable and important to the next incarnation of that soul.

Tibetan Buddhism practices *phowa,* the practice of transferring one's consciousness at the time of death so that the soul of the tulku or lama (a high-ranking and skilled priest) can purposefully wait in a state of unconscious awareness after the life force of his previous body has gone. The tulku or lama can transfer his or her consciousness, experience, wisdom, and connection with the Divine to the next body when he chooses his next manner of rebirth—the time, the place, and the body in which his soul will reside.

As a tulku nears death, he will reveal in signs, omens, and sometimes writings what the signals will be when he is ready to incarnate again. These signs are planned to help the Tibetan priest at the time of his reincarnation determine who the next successor to his lineage is. He will leave a poem or a song about the geographical location where he will be found, information about the parents, a description of the home, and even his physical appearance. There are also prophecies in the Tibetan tradition, spanning generations, that give information about the time and circumstances of the reincarnation of a particular tulku.

When a child is found who is believed to be the next incarnation, he is given various tests to determine if it is indeed the true reincarnation. Ritual objects that belonged to the tulku in a past incarnation will be laid out along with other objects that do not have any connection to him. If the child chooses one or more of the ritual instruments, it is a sign of authenticity, along with the child being able to answer obscure questions correctly that have to do with events in his past life.

I have been using the pronoun "he" to describe the gender of the body—and the majority of the Tibetan priesthood is male—but there are also women tulkus who can be reincarnated. On July 20, 2010, the Dalai Lama was quoted in *Tricycle* magazine as saying that after the death of the body he currently resides within, the next Dalai Lama might not be Tibetan, but may be born in another part of the world and may be female:

> Female Dalai Lama (is) possible because in Tibet tradition, among the high women, reincarnation is there, I think there is the 700–800-year-old Dorjee Phagmo institution which is for female reincarnation . . . so, there is no religious connotation that religious leader must be male.

> If circumstances are such that female reincarnation is more effective to people, then, logically it should be female.

The concept of reincarnation is also the foundation for Hindu spiritual thought. It is part of the structure of the Hindu caste system, wherein the station or status into which one is born is an indication of the evolution of the person's soul. In the spiritual view of some of the more orthodox practicing Hindis, once one has attained birth at a specific status in the caste system, one will always be reborn into that same caste. They believe that it is by living a life that concentrates on the duties and status within the caste one is born into, that dharma (activities, thoughts, and deeds that reflect the natural laws of the universe) is achieved. Other Hindis believe that a reincarnating soul will choose the proper body—whether human, animal, or insect—that will work to further the soul's development and that proper reincarnation is not necessarily linked to a caste or level in society.

In many ancient and modern Native American cultures, from Alaska throughout the lower states, reincarnation is a belief shared as well. As in Hinduism, in much of Native American thought, an incarnating soul could transmigrate into human, animal, or insect form depending on what the soul's purpose was to be within that lifetime. On the continent of Africa, such as in southwest Nigeria and Benin, the Yoruba believe that reincarnation can occur within the family line; that is, individuals can be reincarnated back into the same family. Family members will sometimes name a newborn child *Babatunde* ("father returns") or *Yetunde* ("other returns") if they see a similarity between the newborn and an ancestor in physical appearance or other attributes.

The belief in reincarnation does not exclude Christianity, Islam, or Judaism, either. While the majority of traditions or sects within those religions do not follow the concept of reincarnation as a whole, groups within those spiritual paths do accept reincarnation as a part of the soul's experience. Qabalist Jews, Druze Islamists, and Rosicrucian Christians all hold reincarnation as a part of their spiritual worldview. In fact, reincarnation was accepted by some as a foundation of early Christianity until the belief was condemned by the Second Council of Constantinople in 553 AD.

The physical body that now houses your soul allows your soul to interact with both the physical and spiritual worlds. Your body has physical functions, strengths, limitations, needs, and desires and is a temporary vehicle for your soul and for the distinct personality you possess in this lifetime. This body and its accompanying personality is different with each lifetime that you experience. Your soul uses a different body and a different personality in each lifetime in order to experience as much as possible as it seeks perfection and reconnection with the Divine.

With each incarnation, you are exposed to experiences which can enlighten you and help you to develop knowledge, skills, and gifts that you then bring forward into subsequent incarnations that you experience in physical form. Challenges that you conquer or fail at within a corporeal lifetime each teach you about your soul and its work. When you have met a challenge in a past life with success, thus overcoming a fear or blockage, you gain additional information, experience, and knowledge that you will carry forward in the evolution of your soul's quest—to become one again with the source of all that is.

Challenges that you are faced with in a lifetime (or sometimes again and again in a series of lifetimes) but do not master still teach you much about yourself and your soul. You will have the opportunity over your many incarnations to meet with these challenges again, each time being given the chance to meet them, struggle with them, and overcome them in your evolutionary process.

By the same token, gifts that you are given within a lifetime—a skill such as being able to heal others, a musical talent, the care and nurturing of another—you bring forward into future lives with the ability to use the gift or knowledge again for the benefit and edification of others as you share those parts of yourself with the world.

You have experienced being rich and poor; famous, infamous, and anonymous; male and female (or neuter—one of my lifetimes was in the court of Tzu Hsi, last empress of China, as a lowly eunuch servant—I still feel awe at the sound of her name). You have lived in different parts of the world, spoken different languages, and held a very different view of the world than you do today, now, in this lifetime.

Each incarnation is an experiential teaching lesson for your soul. By meeting and overcoming challenges, you strengthen your core self. In sharing your gifts, you contribute to the beauty and harmony of the world. And by experiencing each incarnation as male or female, rich or poor, educated or uneducated, you experience the world with different eyes and attitudes through the vehicle of that body and personality in that lifetime.

By experiencing life as a wealthy ruler, you have the opportunity to gain skills in leadership, compassion, and empathy when you seek to uplift the people in your care. If, however, you expressed your lifetime as a leader in a negative fashion, being only concerned with your own comfort and welfare, leaving those who were powerless neglected and those who you had responsibility for needy, you did not actualize the gift you were given within that lifetime and will have to make restitution in another life, by serving others and making sure their needs are met. Your actions and reactions to the important experiences of each lifetime create what is known as *karma*, a Sanskrit-based word that means exactly that—reaction to an action. If your reaction to an opportunity to act and make a difference in the world or in the life of an individual is not one that promotes balance, peace, and evolution, you have incurred negative karma and you will need to take action in future lives to bring balance and repay that karmic debt. When you take an action that brings joy to others, promoting their progress and spiritual development, you accrue karmic points to your soul's ledger, and move forward in your own spiritual evolution.

There are billions of souls incarnated in our world now, and these billions have been, like you, a part of the wheel of time and existence from the ancient past and into the present. You have heard the expression "old soul" used to describe a person who acts in the world with good judgment, a steady heart, and an innate knowledge of the importance of creating balance in their life and in the world. An old soul has usually experienced many lifetimes and has retained—sometimes consciously but always unconsciously—the lessons that have been learned and the experiences from events and relationships in past lives.

You have probably also encountered "new souls," people who seem unable to stay centered and focused. They think only of themselves and their own welfare and short-term desires, unaware of the needs of others around them. They are unaware of the fact that we are all spiritual beings incarnated here in physical form and we are all working not only to help our own souls to develop but to aid in this same process for others. However, no matter whether one is an old or a new soul, each one of us is working in our own way to further the evolution of our soul.

Remembering our past lives is a valuable tool that can help to reveal the true direction that our lives should take, tell us what we came to accomplish and, sometimes, with whom we should partner in helping us accomplish our soul's goal. When we understand the goal or purpose of our reincarnation, we know exactly where to apply our time and energy and we are able to move forward in our spiritual evolution with insight and focus. Knowing the circumstances of a death experience, what kind of emotional or karmic ties we may share with another person, or remembering a special gift that we used in a past life, can be freeing and strengthening.

When we know our karma, we can take conscious action in thought, word, and deed to balance the results of an action that we took or a decision that we made in a past life. We can work to balance that energy and uplift ourselves spiritually. Knowing about past relationships with people we are with again today is very helpful, too. Having conscious knowledge about actions that have occurred in past lives allows us to balance the karma with that person and go forward into future lifetimes with those individuals in a positive, clear fashion. Engaging in a past-life experience can also bring comfort and release. If you have fears that seem unfounded in anything you have experienced in this lifetime, those fears may be coming from unconscious past-life memories. Health issues, emotional problems, difficulty connecting with others, feeling as if your success is being snatched away for no apparent reason, all may have connections to your past lives. And when you uncover your past-life experiences and know where some of your unconscious reactions come from, why you have such rocky relationships with some people, or why you have such a fascination with a place, time, or event that doesn't seem to have any connection with who you are now, you can act consciously and confidently to create your future in this and subsequent lives.

One of the real values of a past-life experience and analysis is discovering exactly what type of karmic debt that you came into this lifetime to balance and resolve. According to the teachings of Buddha, the circumstances of one's birth, both fortunate and unfortunate, are the direct result of past-life karma. Every virtuous and nonvirtuous word, thought, emotion, or action creates an energy imprint which at some point will be reflected back as either positive or negative karma. Every action you engage in—mental process, emotional response, physical deed—exerts some type of energy into the universe and results in a consequence. Your thoughts are forms of energy which reach out into the world with resulting reactions. If they are thoughts of peace, balance, and openness, the resulting reaction reflects back to you peace, balance, and openness. If your thoughts are those that brood on any wrong done you, judgmental criticism of others, thoughts that you don't have what it takes to succeed, that is the energy which will result in the same type of reaction from the universe. The energy you send out through your emotions also has consequences—if your emotions contain feelings of love, acceptance, and connection, the resulting reaction in the universe is reflected back to you with that same flavor of energy. However, if your emotional energy is that of fear, repression, envy, and anger, the flavor of energy surrounding you and therefore being attracted back to you will contain that flavor of energy. Certainly your physical world actions, the activities and deeds that you engage in, and the types of goals you work to attain have karmic resultant reactions as well. Actions that you take to bring fulfillment to others, to help to create a world in balance, to activate connection and joy in the people around you all result in reactions that attract back to you the same type of experiences. Actions that you engage in that stymie the work of others or create strife, fear, or control will result in karmic reactions that bring the same type of experience to you.

The karmic results of actions often seem to hold more immediate consequences than the karmic results of mental and emotional energy, but they all work together. When you act, that action is the result of a mental and emotional response to a person or an event, which is then expressed through physical action. Your physical reaction or deed may be an act of conscious determination, or it may be an automatic and unconscious response. By understanding in a conscious fashion exactly what your underlying, unconscious reactions are to different people and circumstances, you empower yourself to make focused, conscious decisions about what actions you really want to take. This decision-making process is what you are working to develop when you investigate your past lives. You want to develop the wisdom to act in accordance with your soul's true purpose, not stumble through this lifetime like a pinball reacting without reflection or knowledge of your true motivations.

Karma is an interesting thing, though. Don't make the mistake of thinking that when you seek to balance your karmic debt that you must interact directly with the individual you may have wronged. If you have the opportunity to redress or resolve a conflict resulting from an action that you took directly with the person or people that you wronged, definitely take that opportunity to create balance and harmony again. But remember, we are all a part of the universe, and we are all connected through our energy patterns and the collective destiny of our souls. There are many times that we indulge in the feelings and thoughts of regret regarding something that we did. Perhaps at the time you thought you were justified in your action for some reason but have since come to understand that you were not and you no longer have a way to contact the person involved who you inadvertently wronged. The way to resolve the karmic energy results is not to continue wallowing in regret, a powerless and pointless exercise. The way to resolve the karmic energy results of your actions is to pay conscious attention to your actions, your thoughts, and your emotions, and when presented with a similar situation, act correctly this time. Try to always use integrity in every action. Monitor your actions, your thoughts, and your emotions in a conscious way, and make sure your actions and reactions come from your soul and its purpose.

When you begin to explore your past lives and the people who were a part of them, you may discover that some of those individuals are sharing part of your life's path with you now. As you uncover the layers of experience and karma that you share with those people, you may find that some of them are family members in this life, a spouse or partner, a friend, or someone who you consider a foe. Sometimes we have a person in our life simply because we find that we work well together or enjoy sharing parts of our lives; sometimes it is because we have a karmic issue that we need to resolve directly with them.

As an example, over thirty years ago a woman I was counseling told me that she had been having difficult problems relating emotionally to her child, and had for some time. The girl was now around seven years old and the mother was taking good care of her, but she had felt an emotional disconnection from the child from birth. The woman had always felt a low level of resentment toward the child and was disturbed that she was not giving the girl the love she deserved. In terms of the rest of the woman's life, she was a happy, successful, and satisfied person with no underlying physical or mental difficulties. I suggested that she look into a possible past-life connection with her daughter to see if that had any bearing on the years-long problem. She scheduled a past-life regression session and what she discovered during the regression was that she and her daughter had experienced a life together in the late 16th century in Le Havre, France, during the time of the Catholic–Huguenot religious wars. They were lovers during that lifetime and the (now) mother had been a young Catholic woman, while her daughter had been a young man and Protestant. During this past life, she had discovered that her Protestant lover had been untrue to her, and in a fit of anger, she betrayed him, resulting in his arrest and death. This experience between the two of them resulted in a karmic debt that the woman now owed her daughter, and which they purposefully came into their present lives to resolve together. The woman now understood that they had agreed in a sacred contract together that they would share a life sometime in the future, wherein the one who was the betrayer would take care of the one who had been betrayed. Once my client understood what the past history had been between them, she felt quite comfortable with her daughter. She understood that coming into this life, she had still carried some of the anger and resentment toward the soul who had became her daughter. By understanding what had happened in the past, and that her role now in their mutual karmic relationship was to nurture and raise this soul into adulthood, she felt clear about what her connection to her child was. She was able to move forward in a positive way, sharing her love and nurturing freely with her daughter. To this day, they are close and have a very good relationship.

I mentioned "sacred contracts," and you may wonder what I am referring to. A sacred contract is an agreement you make with your soul, usually between lifetimes, regarding experiences you want to have in a future life that will help your soul's evolution. The knowledge of this sacred contract is held in the unconscious mind and results in a feeling within you that there is something very important that you are meant to do or achieve in this lifetime. The knowledge of this contract resides in your unconscious self, and you may act unknowingly upon its direction and purpose in your daily life through your responses to people and events. Sometimes during the process of being birthed into another physical body, and with the distractions of learning to use that body, you forget what your spiritual intentions were coming into this life. Until you bring the contents of your sacred contract into your conscious life, you won't necessarily see the bigger picture of what you intended to fulfill this time around. This sacred contract can be a pact that you made simply with your own soul, or it can involve other souls who are incarnating into this time and in close proximity to you. When you understand what your contract contains, you can move forward very clearly and purposefully. You can work consciously with those other incarnated souls to be partners in each other's soul development.

This possible soul connection can be a tricky business, however, and you don't want to fall prey to wishful thinking that you are "supposed" to be with another person, that they are your soul mate and your destinies are intrinsically and irrevocably intertwined. The emotional baggage that can be created by the concept of a soul mate can be detrimental to your soul's progress if you use it unwisely, in a delusional fashion, or work to create energy bonds with other people that are inappropriate and imprisoning. Your soul is sometimes working from a different perspective and with a different intended goal than what your conscious mind perceives and desires at a given moment in time. What the soul seeks to do is expand and fulfill its purpose of connection with the Divine, not provide you with a lover who will travel with you throughout time and in each life. The popular concept of a soul mate sometimes seems to me to have the connotations associated with plots in gothic romance novels—that two ill-fated lovers were parted in a past life only to be reunited in a current life, and their bonds should not and cannot be severed, come high water and fury. Don't fall prey to this type of constricted belief, or the bonds you create or act upon with people will not be healthy and the relationship will impede your spiritual progress.

We meet and engage with many different souls throughout each lifetime and each one gives us an experience or a lesson which can enrich our evolution if we take it in the proper context. Even those people who give us the harshest lessons are giving us valuable experience, knowledge, and wisdom that, if we use that lesson appropriately and with the development of our soul in mind, are actually giving us a gift—a gift of perspective, as well as an opportunity to act from universal soul and to keep our karmic lessons clear.

Every day, from our most mundane acts to those of the most profound spiritual inspiration, we create karma by the energy of our acts, which can be intentional and unintentional. Unintentional actions create karma from the results of those actions, but it is one's intention that largely determines the weight of the karmic results. For example, if your motivation comes from a place of compassion and empathy when you help someone else rather than from a sense of duty or self-interest, it is a spiritually pure motivation and the karmic reaction created is more positively weighted. Likewise, a premeditated harmful action bears more karmic results than a harmful action that was impulsive. There is still a resolution that must happen in that instance, and energy was released from the action which needs to be balanced, but not as much as consciously intended harm. Thus, the purer the motivation, positive or negative, the stronger the manifestation of the karma.

If we are unaware of experiences from our past lives and therefore how we are influenced in this lifetime by those events, we may feel that many times difficulties seem to come out of nowhere. Responding to difficulties by complaining, blaming, or deciding that we are powerless in our life—particularly when specific types of difficulties occur that seem to confront us again and again—is a negative response to the already negative karma manifesting from our past. That kind of response creates even more negative karma. When we are having difficulties, a more consciously spiritual reaction is to accept the situation as it is while committing to changing the way we are expressing our energies. We need to recognize that it is the karmic reaction to our actions from the past that is creating the present problems. We should not have harsh thoughts or actions towards ourselves or anyone else regarding the matter. We create positive karma when we respond positively to the negative. Many times this can also clear the effect of the particular negative karma.

And when we are experiencing the effects of positive karma—when things are going well in our lives—we should use the time to further develop our spiritual expression, connection, and balance, so that when we are faced with difficult challenges again, we will have developed the ability to respond with more acceptance and patience. You have this potential at every moment of your life.

Information about our past lives can be useful to release subconscious blockages, to understand our interactions with important people in our current life, to bring to fruition untapped talents, and to simply know more about yourself and your spiritual journey. If you are curious about your past lives and what kind of direct bearing they may have on this present life, experiment with the following exercises.

EXERCISE 28: PAST-LIFE RECALL MIRROR TECHNIQUE

This exercise may be one of my favorite methods for initiating past-life recall. The results are quick, often surprising, and easy to obtain.

Your tools for this exercise are:

✧ Journal and pen

✧ Two purple candles (purple is a color that aids in making psychic and spiritual connections)

✧ A mirror on a stand

✧ A small table with a chair for you to sit on

✧ Oil or incense composed of scents that open your psychic faculties, like wisteria, white sandalwood, jasmine, or neroli (optional)

✧ Incense burner (optional)

✧ Recorder (optional)

As with all of your psychic work, select a time and place when you will not be disturbed or distracted. Be sure that you plan your experience so that you will have quiet and privacy; unplug the phone, make sure the pets are fed and contained in a space away from you, and take care of any other possible interruptions. Do not eat much this day: fruits and raw vegetables, very little coffee or other stimulants, and no alcohol or any other mind-altering substances. You want your body and mind to be clear so that you know the information you receive is not influenced by any outside effect.

Have a journal and pen ready to write information and impressions or set up a recorder if you think you would prefer to speak aloud about the information you receive. Even if you plan to use a recorder, plan to also create a past-life diary so that as additional information comes through in the days after your initial work, you have a place to keep a record. When you listen to the recording later and transcribe the experience in your diary, you will probably have more information hits as you write.

Set up a table large enough that you can sit at it in a chair and with enough surface area to set your candles, the mirror on a stand, and an incense burner or oil if you are using either one or both in your work tonight.

If you are using incense in your work, place the incense burner to the side of the table where you will receive the benefit of the scent without having the smoke blowing into your eyes and throat.

If you are using an oil to facilitate the opening of your psychic senses, place the oil bottle on the table within easy reach so that you don't distract yourself trying to locate it on the table when you are ready to use it.

Set the standing mirror in the center of the table at a distance from you that allows you to see into it clearly without straining your body. The candles should be to the sides of the mirror and a few inches behind it so that you have illumination, but the candle flames do not reflect in the mirror. Place your journal within reach, or if you are using a recorder, make sure that it is ready to go.

Light the candles and then your incense if you choose to use it as a tool to deepen your experience. Anoint your Third Eye (just above and between your eyebrows) with any of the

continued on the next page

continued from the previous page

suggested oils or a blend of some of those oils if you want to use your sense of smell to help you in your work.

Begin with your meditative breath—deep and slow as you ground your energies, connecting them with those of the earth. Once you have linked your energy field with that of the earth, draw energy up from that source and bring it up through your body with each breath. Continue to breathe in this energy from the earth and extend it into your auric field, out past your body, creating a circle of energy and light to surround you at your table.

Settle back in your chair quietly, keeping your spine straight but relaxed. Continue breathing slowly and deeply. With each exhalation, feel all stress and nervousness flow out of your body. With each inhalation, feel your body become heavier and more relaxed. Breathe in this manner until your legs feel very heavy, almost physically connected to the earth and to your chair, and you feel mentally relaxed and focused. If you are using a recorder, begin recording.

Gazing at your face in the mirror, let your eyes unfocus slightly, resting their gaze in the center of your face's reflection in the mirror but not concentrating on any one facial feature. After a very short while (so long as you stay mentally and physically relaxed) you will find that the face in the mirror begins to morph, to change sometimes just slightly, sometimes dramatically. You may notice the hair around the face is different as well or has a hat, garland, or crown on it. You may also notice that the new face in the mirror is a different gender, culture, or age than you are currently.

As you see your face changing, do not allow your mind to shock your consciousness back to a normal beta-state by being surprised. Just relax into the changes and ask yourself, either silently or out loud, "What is the name?" Continue asking questions regarding place, time, relatives, the karmic lesson to be learned from this life, etc.

You may find that during one session your face may change several times, or it may stay with just the first change. If you have several changes, with each change, ask the questions to get information about the identity, place, and time of each face. When the face in the mirror changes back to the one you have in this life, or you become tired, begin writing down all of your impressions and the answers to your questions if your are journaling to record the experience.

When you are finished, put out your candles and use them later only for this same ritual. You will need to either go immediately to bed or ground yourself thoroughly by eating a meal. You may find that in addition to the past-life recall experience you just had that you also get additional information in the dreams you have in the next few nights. You may also find that you get more information as you are occupied in your day-to-day life—while driving, eating lunch, gazing out the window, you will often suddenly get another piece of information. Add this bit to your journal and note where you were and what you were doing when the information came.

You may find that the first few times you do this you get your best results by using the planetary energies and moon phase as part of your planning by performing the work on a Monday (day of the Moon and the subconscious) or Saturday

continued on the next page

continued from the previous page

(day of Saturn and understanding karma) during the waning phase of the moon, when the subconscious mind tends to be more active.

EXERCISE 29: SELF-HYPNOSIS USING SCRYING

This technique is helpful when you have experienced an intense interest or fascination with a time in history, a geographical area, a particular culture, or have a strong feeling that there is an energy connection between you and another person. As with Exercise 28, you will have your past-life journal at the ready, or the recorder ready to go

For this work, you can use a crystal ball, a scrying mirror, a medium to large piece of quartz crystal, moonstone, or labradorite or some other object which will be used as a focal point for relaxed concentration. As usual, create a serene environment for yourself where you will not be interrupted or distracted. Begin your meditative breath and ground your energies with that of the earth and bring those energies up and out of your body, filling your aura and the space with a soothing, light energy.

Hold your scrying object in your hands or have it placed by itself on a table where you can comfortably focus your attention, keeping your body relaxed and your spine straight. Align your energies with that of your scrying object and begin meditating on the time in history, the geographical place, the culture, or the individual with whom you feel the energy connection. You may just allow yourself to drift within your mind for a time as you meditate in this fashion. Allow images to come forward in your mind or claircognizant pieces of information to be revealed to you. Or, you may choose to start the session by asking aloud or in your mind, "What is my connection to this time, to this place, to this person?" After asking the question, simply sit back and relax while allowing the information to come forward.

As you receive each piece of information, state it aloud for the recorder or jot down a few key words about what you are getting. Always ask aloud what name you were called in that lifetime so that you have an easy reference point to come back to later, when you want to begin more investigation into that lifetime. As you receive images or bits of knowing, always ask "'What is the importance of this piece?" so that you can steer your work in a direction that gives you the information you are seeking. At first, your purpose may simply be to have the experience, but once you are confident in that, the real work becomes discovering what aspects of that past life are influencing you now.

EXERCISE 30: PAST-LIFE ACCESS WITH YOUR SPIRIT GUIDE

Once you have established a relationship with, and connection to, your spirit guide, you may wish to enlist their help in receiving information regarding lives you have experienced in the past. Prepare yourself in the usual way using your meditative breath and light meditation. Picture your guide in your mind or call out to them aloud or psychically. When they are there and connected with you, ask "What experience or lesson from a past life is important for me to become aware of right now?" or "Show me a past life that contains information that I should know." You will receive a clairaudient message or lesson that gives you the information that you are seeking, or a series of mental images showing you the important events you should be considering in terms of issues you are facing at this time. Just as in any past-life work, if the lifetime and body is one you have not been aware of previously, ask specific questions regarding the name, the place, and the time so that you have tools you can use in the future if you want to connect with this lifetime again.

One of the hallmarks of having a dream about a past life is that in the dream, you know that it is you, but you look different (in age, gender, or race) as you observe the events happening in the dream. You may be observing yourself as the events unfold in the dream, or you may be observing the events through the eyes of the person in the dream, but in either case you are aware that it is you. Many times in our past-life recall dream state, we reexperience a traumatic event or a death experience. What is happening at these times is that your higher self—your soul self—is teaching you that there is nothing to fear from death, and that any trauma that you have experienced in the past, or will experience in this present life, is a temporary thing.

Usually when you are having a dream that is just about your present life, you tend to see yourself as others see you now—your usual daily appearance. You feel as if you are living the dream from inside your current body. In past-life dreams, the feeling you have very markedly is that the figure you see is you but you see yourself with a different physical appearance. You are a different age, in a very clear location or environment, and sometimes with a different gender or race. You have a different personality, belief system, and attitude toward the world around you.

When I was around nineteen years of age, I had a very vivid dream in which I was walking through a large house at night. I felt apprehensive and was trying to be very quiet. I was watching myself in the dream and I knew emphatically that it was me. I was a black man around the age of thirty or so with ragged clothing, a rope belt, and knotty hair. I was carrying a satchel that was empty, and I was looking around for things of value that I could put in it. As I rounded the corner by the staircase, I heard my name called loudly, "Jess!" and I looked up. At that instant, a shotgun went off in my face—the light from the explosion blinding me. As I fell to the floor I knew I was dead and my response was one of wonder and curiosity. The noise from the shotgun in my dream awakened me from my sleeping state. I lay in bed still in a half-dream haze and began to go over the dream events in my head. I knew that it had been a dream of a past life, the feelings were so intense during the experience. I asked what was going on in that dream and received a knowing that I had been a slave on a farm in Missouri and that I had decided to escape and take my chances at freedom. I had snuck into the master's house to steal some things that I might be able to sell to buy food and transportation during my escape journey, but was unfortunately discovered and killed by my master. What did I learn from this past-life dream? That the experience of death doesn't really hurt and it doesn't end the essence of your soul or your existence.

You may have an experience in which you have very distinct dreams about a time in history or a place or country somewhere in the world that in this present life you don't know much about. If this dream is sequential in its actions and logical in its presentation of the events that are happening, this is possibly a past-life dream showing you experiences that you had at that time and in that place—in your dream state you are experiencing a past-life memory. These types of dreams tend to be recurring. You may have a time in your life when you have a particular dream again and again over a short period of time. If you were not aware of the existence of past lives at the time, you may have simply decided that it was an interesting series of dreams. But what was really happening was that your subconscious mind was trying to give you information about something from your past that had a bearing on something you were encountering at that time in your present life.

Or you may experience a dream that is unusually intense—the events happening in the dream are very clear and follow a script that is logical and sequential, unlike many dreams that seem to have no sense and bounce from scene to scene without direction or a point.

You may be speaking another language, which in the dream is perfectly understandable to you, but upon awakening you no longer understand what was being said. In a dream, you may know the main character is yourself, but your worldview, attitude, and beliefs within the dream are nothing like who you are today. When you find yourself dreaming vividly about particular times in history, perhaps historical people, events, places, and things, there is a good chance that you are linking into a past life that contains information that is important to something you are doing now.

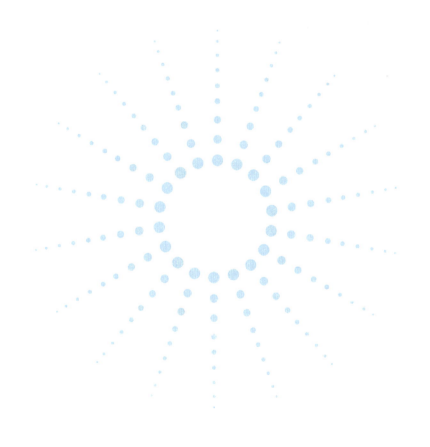

For this exercise, you may want to create a dream chamber in the fashion of ancient civilizations like Greece to prepare an environment totally conducive to your experience. You may want to make or purchase some sleeping attire that you wear only when you are doing this type of work—the feel of the material against your skin will be a sensory reminder to your subconscious of the specific type of work you do when you wear it, and it will serve as a part of your conscious preparations for any dream work you do now and in the future. The fabric should be soft and light with little or no decoration and the fit should be loose. You will be using the light from one candle in this exercise, blue (inducing tranquility), white (purifying the atmosphere), or purple (connecting with the psyche and the Divine), so you will need to decide what flavor of energy will be most conducive to the work you are doing. You can use a taper candle (usually six to ten inches long and held by a standard candle holder), a votive candle in a cup, or a seven-day candle contained in a cylindrical glass holder, typically the same height as the seven-day candle.

Prior to beginning your dream work, you may also wish to drink a tea composed of jasmine and lavender flowers. The jasmine will relax you and arouse your subconscious mind, while the lavender flowers will help with your memories and allow your body and mind to drift in a serene state.

Lay out some bedclothes that are soft and nonbinding. Take a hot shower or bath to encourage your body to fully relax and release any tensions, to remove toxins from your body, and to cleanse your aura of any extraneous energy from your day-to-day life. As you bathe, bathe with intention, breathing in light and relaxation and exhaling any stress, distraction, or tension within your body and your mind. As you bathe, determine your dream intention: revisit a past life that you are aware of and have some information about from previous visitations, or uncover a lifetime and existence that will be a new memory for you but has pertinent information for you at this time.

After bathing, go to your dream chamber or your bedroom and dress yourself in your chosen attire. Lay your journal by the bedside along with a writing utensil easily at hand. Light your blue, white, or purple candle, then extinguish all other light. Lie down and begin your usual meditative breath and light energy meditation as you ground your energies with that of the earth. As you begin to drift into sleep, focus on your intention for the evening. If your intention is to revisit a lifetime you have come to before in a meditation or working, visualize in your mind your appearance in that lifetime, any important landscape you feel affinity to, or other clues to memories that you have connected to that life.

Upon awakening, record in your journal the retrieved memories of the dream and leave additional space in case there is other information that comes to you over the next few days after the experience.

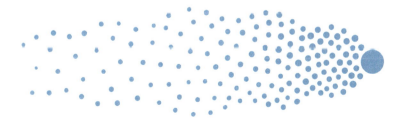

CHAPTER 7

Automatic Writing

Automatic writing (also known as psychography) is a form of mediumship whereby writings are produced while the practitioner is in a light trance (alpha) state, having deliberately set aside their conscious, linear mind. Automatic writing is the process, or product, of writing material that does not come from the conscious thoughts of the writer, but from a deeper source within or a spiritual source outside of the individual. Psychography seems to be a relatively recent phenomenon of the last one hundred years.

There are varying opinions about how automatic writing takes place. Some people feel that it comes out of the subconscious mind of the writer as they purposefully allow their higher self to communicate freely without the critic in the conscious mind impeding the process. Others explain the experience of automatic writing as a process in which the writing comes from a spiritual source such as a spirit guide, a person who has passed away, or an angelic presence, without the conscious awareness or interference by the writer. In my experience, it can be both. Automatic writing can be done with the assistance of spirit to receive messages, information, and inspiration, but it can also often be used to directly access the subconscious mind of an individual to retrieve answers and memories from deep within. If you have done any writing, drawing, or music composition, you have likely experienced this process when you have allowed yourself to move into the flow of creative energy and let the information, images, or sequences of musical notes give voice to themselves through the medium of your hands and your subconscious mind. Your fingers fly over the computer keyboard, the paper, or the musical instrument under their own volition, and you find yourself astonished at the craft of your work.

In recent history, famed writer William Butler Yeats and his wife Georgie Hyde-Lees witnessed the power of automatic writing. After a tumultuous courtship, Hyde-Lees married Yeats and began to experiment with automatic writing only days later. Although rambling and fragmentary, the writing became the foundation for Yeats' book, *A Vision,* of which he published two versions, one in 1925 and a revised edition in 1937. Yeats took the fragments of thoughts, theories, and philosophies that his wife accessed during automatic writing sessions and expanded them into a detailed and expansive study of esoteric topics encompassing history, philosophy, astrology, poetry, and hermetic thought. *A Vision* brought together these divergent ideas and subjects into a working system that expounded on the nature of reality and the workings of the universe.

Yeats said of the collaborative nature of his work with his wife:

> On the afternoon of October 24th 1917, four days after my marriage, my wife surprised me by attempting automatic writing. What came in disjointed sentences, in almost illegible writing, was so exciting, sometimes so profound, that I persuaded her to give an hour or two day after day to the unknown writer, and after some half-dozen such hours offered to spend what remained of life explaining and piecing together those scattered sentences. "No," was the answer, "we have come to give you metaphors for poetry."
>
> —INTRODUCTION TO *A VISION* FROM *A PACKET FOR EZRA POUND,*
> *A VISION* (LONDON: MACMILLAN, 1962)

Another example of recent automatic writing is that of the book series *Conversations with God* by Neale Donald Walsch. Walsch relates that during a troubled time in his life, he began writing down questions to God. In response he received channeled messages through the process of automatic writing from God in answer to the written questions he posed to the Divine. Walsch would write down a question, allow his consciousness to open and expand while allowing his hand to be guided to write the Divine answer. These answers became the book. First published in 1995, *Conversations with God* has become a nine-book series and book one was on the *New York Times* bestseller list for 137 weeks.

In the activity of automatic writing, as in all psychic skills, you alter your energy flow and the nature of your consciousness to that of the alpha or theta state and move your conscious mind (and the critic that your conscious mind often displays) out of the way, allowing departed spirits, guides, or your higher self (that part of yourself which transcends the basic intellectual and emotional components of your personality and connects you directly to the spiritual realm) to be given expression through the vehicle of writing. This writing can occur with a pen or pencil, a typewriter, or a computer keyboard.

When using automatic writing, you step back on a conscious level and allow your subconscious spirit to take control of your hands to write messages, letters, and even entire books. Depending on the medium, automatic writing can be done while in a completely unconscious trance, or in a meditative waking state. In a trance (theta) state, the muscles and mechanics of the writer's hand will form the message (or the picture—automatic writing can encompass automatic drawing of images as well), while you remain unaware of what is being written. In a more conscious, yet meditative, alpha state, you are aware of your surroundings and the actions of your writing hand, but are simply providing the vehicle for getting the thoughts, messages, or wisdom on paper.

The process of automatic drawing is the same as automatic writing. In the early 20th century, the ideas and automatic mediumship of the French psychic Hélène Smith greatly influenced the Surrealist art movement. A medium through the technique of automatic writing, she was known as the "Muse of the Surrealists" through her association with many of the artists of that influential artistic genre. André Breton, founder of the Surrealist movement, believed that artistic expression and images exist within the subconscious mind and that the use of trance and altered conscious states, (what he called "pure psychic automatism") was the way to capture artistic inspiration and manifest it physically in a picture, sculpture, or writing. Automatic writing and drawing became an active part of a Surrealistic artist's way of gaining access to the subconscious for inspiration and creativity. In the work of other Surrealist artists, such as Salvador Dalí and Joan Miró, you can see the connection between the artists' subconscious minds and the spirit world in the images portrayed.

Here are some exercises that you can use to experiment with the process of automatic writing or drawing for yourself.

EXERCISE 32: PRACTICE AUTOMATIC WRITING

As with any of the things that you are doing to discover and strengthen your psychic senses and abilities, choose a time and a place where you know that you will not be interrupted or disturbed. For the best results, you need a sense of calm and privacy as you experiment.

First, begin by slowing your breathing and grounding your energies. Clear your mind of any extraneous thoughts and allow your body to completely relax. Take a pen or pencil in your hand and place the writing tip against the surface of a piece of paper as if you are about to write something. Or sit at your computer and open a new document in your word processing program. Turn your attention to something else in the room—watching birds out of a window, listening to a radio program, gazing to the side of the room or simply daydreaming. As you relax, you may have the sensation that your hands are being gently guided or that you are writing down dictation—you are acting as a stenographer for spirit or something deep within yourself.

The automatic writing may come in just a few words or sentences, or whole paragraphs may appear. Often, when you are writing by hand, the writing is illegible and hard to read. The text may appear jumbled and contain misspellings or improper grammar and punctuation. Many times, when there are sentences or paragraphs, they will be rambling, composed of mostly run-on sentences and concepts. Let all of the information simply flow—don't engage your conscious mind to think about or criticize anything that you are writing. Just keep

continued on the next page

continued from the previous page

writing. Do not allow time for your conscious mind to listen to or read the information you are getting. Just continue to type or write until you feel that it is finished.

Messages can often be written in a language style or handwriting style that is not recognized by the writer. Some automatic writers know who is giving the messages, while others do not. If the energies feel comfortable to you, then you will soon learn who the entity is and why it is writing with you. If you are writing by hand, you may find that you have drawn a symbol or picture as part of the message. As the energy connection between you and the spirit guide is made, ask for the name of the guide as well as the signal they will use to let you know they are ready to work with you. This signal can be anything from a clairvoyant image, a scent, a clairaudient sound such as a bell or musical note, or a physical sensation of buzzing around the head. This will allow you to know to whom you are speaking and addressing questions in the future, and will help you develop a relationship for contact. If at any time during the session you feel uncomfortable with the experience, stop and reground yourself, releasing any energy connection you have made.

If the experience feels negative, angry, fearful, or heavy, you're not bringing through a source that you want to tap into and allow to use your body. You do not want to develop a connection or a relationship with any disembodied entity that causes you to feel uncomfortable, just as you would not with a physical person.

As you develop an automatic writing relationship with a spirit guide or your higher self, begin with simple yes or no questions. To test the validity of the answer, you may want to experiment with asking a question that you don't currently know the answer to, but that you can get outside verification about. After you receive some yes and no answers, do a little research on whether the yes or no answer was correct. As your relationship deepens, you can begin asking questions that are beyond yes or no answers and get more detailed responses. You may ask questions about your spiritual work, in what areas you can most easily develop your talents, or where you should be putting focus in your life.

After you have had a good working relationship for a month or two, and have taken the time and effort to verify the answers to questions you have asked in this developmental period, you will be ready to trust your guide to give you good answers to anything that may be troubling you. The guidance that you receive should be very clear, and feel light. It will usually be expressed in straightforward, simple terms and will comfort you, provide clarity within a situation, or raise your emotional level to one of confidence and well-being.

If you have already created a relationship with a spirit guide or a person who is no longer living, you may want to use automatic writing as a way to make contact with them. In this case, you will begin your session with the usual slow, meditative breath and grounding, get yourself settled at your writing desk and open your energies to your guide, calling upon your guide in the way that the two of you have established. Then write or type a question. Again, do not focus your attention on your hands, the paper, the computer keyboard, or monitor. Allow your conscious mind to relax and retreat into a gentle distraction out of the window or within a daydream. You will feel your hands begin to work and may also receive spirit dictation that you will begin to transcribe.

It is important that, during the automatic writing session, you do not allow your conscious mind to read or interpret the information you're receiving. After the session ends, you will interpret what you received using both your psychic senses and your conscious mind. If you engage the conscious mind during the process, you will throw your brain activity back into the linear, conscious mind beta state and lose the psychic connection.

If you have more than one guide, and you begin to feel that more than one entity is trying to write through you, request that only one work with you at a time. Let them know that you will allow everyone who has something to contribute make that contribution, but just one at a time.

You will not always receive the answer that you hoped for. In these cases, the next question to ask is what you need to do to help the situation you are asking about come to a more positive conclusion.

Can you utilize the skills of automatic writing on the behalf of others? Of course! While we have been talking about using automatic writing to get answers for yourself or to engage the subconscious mind and the higher self for inspiration, creativity, and wisdom, you can employ the same techniques to help another person to receive answers from their guides or subconscious mind. When working on behalf of another, you will prepare yourself to enter a meditative, alpha mind state or a trance-like theta state, just as you do when you are working with yourself.

Once you are grounded, centered, and open, the client should address a question to Spirit out loud. You will wait with writing utensil in hand, and allow spirit to flow through you, giving the answer or message in response to the question. Sometimes you may not be in physical proximity to your client—they may be in another part of town or even in another state. In this case, the client will have provided you with the questions that they would like answers to via letter, email, or a phone call. You will select a time and place to do the work, read the questions, purposefully put yourself in an altered state of psychic awareness, and begin to receive and write answers.

Again, you may receive answers that are fragmentary—a word, an incomplete sentence—or you may find yourself writing paragraphs. During the session do not read what you are writing, but do take note of any emotions, physical sensations, images, scents, or tastes that come along with the writing. Sometimes, after the session when you are back in your normal, beta brain state, the information you received will not make complete sense to you. Don't worry about it—when you convey the information to your client you will usually have the gratifying experience of having them confirm the messages that you received. The image that you had of the hallway door while you were writing will have meaning to the client. The seemingly cryptic sentence, "It was in the spring" will make perfect sense to the person for whom you are doing the reading. And, oftentimes, as you transcribe the messages while in a more conscious state, additional information will flow to you about the answer or circumstance that will flesh out what first appeared to be nonsensical.

CHAPTER 8

Psychometry: Sensing and Interpreting Energy in Objects and Places

Psychometry, when translated from Greek, means "measure of the soul." Psychometry is a form of psychic ability that allows one to read an object's residual psychic energy through the handling of that object. Typically, this object is held in the hands as the psychic opens their psychic senses to the information that resides within the energy field of the object. This information is contained within the energy patterns left on the physical object and its auric field by the person who now owns or once owned the object—a sort of psychic imprint of the person's attitudes, thoughts, personality, and feelings as well as the ways that the individual tends to interact in their lives and environment. In addition to holding objects and interacting with the energy residing in an object to obtain answers, the art of dowsing and the use of the pendulum are forms of psychometry as well. We'll examine how dowsing rods and pendulums can be used to get information later in this chapter.

Whenever we physically interact with anything by wearing it, writing with it, carrying it with us, or using it to help us accomplish any work or creative project, we leave a bit of psychic energy residue behind in the energy of that thing. Objects within a home (furniture, art objects, kitchen utensils) are infused with the owner's energy as well. It is an object's continued use, being in the presence of, or worn by, a person that imprints energy patterns within the auric field of the object. The analysis of the psychometric energy flavors in a reading acts as an aid to the psychic, helping him or her tune into their client more clearly by creating a smooth energy link while utilizing the thing in what is called an object link. While a psychic may choose to simply receive random information while handling the object, specific questions can be asked during a psychometric session as well, and the energy impressions picked up by the psychic will give information and answers to those questions. These can be simple yes or no questions or they can be broader in scope.

Many psychics who use psychometric techniques tend to prefer to use metal objects such as rings, bracelets, or other types of jewelry. These objects have often been in contact with the person on a regular basis and therefore will retain more energy and information about that person. But any object can be read psychometrically: articles of clothing worn by a person are full of the individual's energy residue, as are photographs of the person, or letters written and drawings created by that person. All of these things will have a strong energy link to them. There are no rules about which objects should or must be used for the psychic contact and reading, it's simply a matter of what works best for the individual psychic and their use of whatever object link is available to them in the reading.

Let's begin playing with your psychometric sense by taking advantage of the frequency vibrations contained within colors. As you know, after your reading of the chapter concerning auras and color, our perception of a color, its hue, tint, or saturation, is due to the vibrational frequency that each color contains and consists of. Each shade is perceived as the color we see because the energy within it, or the color that saturates its surface, moves at a particular and specific vibrational speed that interacts with a light source. In our first exercise, you will learn to identify what the energy frequency of a color feels like.

EXERCISE 33: SENSING THE VIBRATIONAL ENERGY IN COLOR

You will need:

✦ Magazines with colorful photos and/or fabric swatches

✦ Scissors

✦ Opaque envelopes

From pictures in a color magazine, cut two-inch, square pieces of different solid colors. Or, if you have access to fabric swatches, cut two-inch, square pieces of solidly colored material from differently colored swatches. Taking up one piece at a time, focus your concentration on a colored square. One by one, gaze at the color of the paper or fabric, then place it between your palms. Fill your mind with the hue of that color. Now open your perceptions and delve into the feel of the piece. Note what type of sensations you get. Do you get a feeling of temperature? A feeling of solidity or a buzzy movement? Is it fluid or static? Make a mental note of how that color feels to you and what types of images or feelings the color evokes in you. Also note what types of psychic body sensations the color conveys to you—do you feel lighter when handling that color? Do you feel heavier, clearer, more energized, or calmer? Make a physical note of how that color feels to you.

After experiencing each color's energy signature, place each of the squares of colored paper or fabric in a separate opaque envelope. Shuffle the envelopes around so that your conscious mind does not know which envelope contains which color. Pick an envelope at random and place one palm under the envelope and one on top of it. Relax and sit quietly as you open your sensitivity to the feeling of the energy of the

continued on the next page

continued from the previous page

color within the envelope. Allow your mind to be relaxed yet focused, and close your eyes. Before you open the envelope to see the color physically, first sense with your own auric field what the color in the envelope feels like. Is it buzzy? Hot? Cool? Bright? Fluid? You may receive a knowing within your mind as to the color, or you may see within your mind's eye a color. Open the envelope and see if the feelings you received when you couldn't see the color match up with your initial impressions of the energy of the color when you could physically see it. Repeat this exercise until you can correctly identify the color swatch within the envelope with the vibrational feel of the color in your body and your mind's eye.

EXERCISE 34: SENSING THE ENERGY OF OBJECTS

You can perform a similar exercise with the energy feeling of objects.

You will need:

- ✧ Rectangular box that is approximately five by seven inches

- ✧ Four to six objects that will fit inside the box and are similar in weight but different in constitution. For example, a nail, a stone or crystal, a clump of feathers, a small vial of water, a piece of velvet, and a book of matches

❖ Cotton balls or tissue paper (enough to line the bottom of the box)

Find a rectangular box that is about five by seven inches or so. As noted above, select four to six objects that will fit in the box and are similar in weight but different in constitution. You don't want to have objects that weigh measurably more or less than one another—otherwise your conscious mind will interfere and try to guess what object is in the box. Line the box with some cotton balls or layers of tissue paper so that whatever is placed within the box will not rattle around to give your conscious mind hints. Just as you did with the color swatches, handle each object one by one, looking at it with your physical eyes and handling it with your hands while feeling the energy emanations of the object. Next, have a friend go into a different room, place one of the objects in the box, and bring it back to you. Relax, open your senses to the object in the box, and feel what the major basic elemental energy of the object presents to you about its physical make-up. Does it have a feeling of solid mass? Does it feel sharp? Does it feel light and airy? Does it present the feeling of fluidity to you or feel soft? Does it bring any mental psychic images to your mind? After you have gotten a sense of physical presence and energy from the object, open the box and see how open your senses were to its identity.

Psychometric energy reception and analysis can also be part of how a psychic receives information when they are using other psychic tools such as tarot cards or rune stones. In these cases, the person who is receiving the reading physically handles the cards or the stones as they consider their question. As the querent is focusing their energy and attention on their question while shuffling the tarot deck or warming the rune stones with the heat of their hands, they are imbuing that physical psychic tool with their own energy signature. And, as it so often happens in psychic work, the person who is asking the question can also be the source of the answer to the question they are asking. This information is held within the person's own subconscious mind, and as they focus on their concern, they are also adding that information regarding the answer to the energy store within the psychic device.

Many times, when a person receives a psychic reading, they already know the answer to their question in their own subconscious mind, and the reading is simply a confirmation of what they already know, not an unexpected revelation to them. The employment of any psychic skill is an act of accessing the subconscious mind of both the reader and the client to bring to conscious attention the energy surrounding a question or concern, and the direction in which the querent's energy is taking the events.

Whenever we handle something that is physical, we are laying down information about ourselves on and within that object with our own energy field. Our bodies give off magnetic energy all of the time. This psychic energy transfer can be likened to recording a voice or music onto magnetic audiotape. You could think of the psychic as being like a tape player that is set up to receive the vibrational frequencies of sound infused onto the tape during the recording process. When a psychic opens their senses and their skills to the energy presences within a thing, they are playing back the information stored in the energy field of the object. There is a lot of psychic information contained within the energy field of any object, and, using the audiotape analogy, while the psychic is employing their skills, they are accessing specific information to answer a question. By asking a direct question, they can find the specific information within the object they are reading by tuning in to the emotions, experiences, and memories contained within its energy field, just like a specific song can be located on the tape.

One thing to keep in mind when you use psychometry is that an object may have been handled intimately by more than one person during its existence, thus its history may reveal layers of information about things that are not relevant to the direct question at hand. If, for example, an object has been passed down through generations to different members within a family, it will contain information about all of its previous owners as well as the person who has it now. Obtaining information from such an object can be interesting and helpful in investigating the family's history as a whole, but specific and direct questions will need to be used to get clear answers to questions regarding that specific individual.

As the psychic works with the object, the information is received or picked up by their subconscious mind. The energy flavors or signatures on objects are expressed to the psychic via the mental images they receive, emotional impressions that they get, the clairaudient messages they hear, and knowledge they receive via claircognizant knowing. The imprints left on objects can relate to any form of information: a location, a time, a feeling, an event. All of these psychic imprints or impressions are stored within the energy field of an object and can be accessed by the psychic senses.

A reader may choose to start with psychometry at the beginning of a reading, to help make a quick and clear link into the person with whom they are working psychically. This energy connection will help to bring forth some basic sense about that particular person, and also help the person being read to open their energies to the psychic, thus joining the two in the session in a receptive energy link. This adds to the clarity and accuracy of the information that is being accessed. When you are working directly with a person who is providing you with a physical object as an energy link to them, begin by asking them to take off their ring, pendant, watch or whatever the object may be, and hand it to you. This is the beginning of the energy link, as they move their auric field into yours while handing you the object. Next, ask the person you are about to read for if you have their permission to read for them. At their assent, the link has been connected between you and your client and you can confidently start the session.

While you are holding an object belonging to a client, begin by relaxing and slowing your breath. Close your eyes and let the energy of the object connect with you. As you handle it, feel its physicality—its texture, weight, and shape. Allow the feeling of the physical presence of the object to become imprinted in your mind. Open to the feelings that the energy of the object link is beginning to communicate to you. Imagine information flowing to you, entering through your fingertips, traveling up your arm, and entering your thoughts. Create an energy stream between yourself and the object. At first, you will see or feel just bits of information: a sudden flash of a scene, an emotion, a fleeting memory. Mention all the impressions you are receiving. Say out loud what you are seeing and sensing, and tell your client that it would be helpful to your work if they would confirm information you are stating and tell you when a piece of information does not seem to have any connection to the question being asked.

As you get feedback from the person you are working with, you will undoubtedly get some information wrong. This is normal and is part of your training process. Sometimes, in our eagerness to get information or our impatience with the process, fledgling psychics try to flesh out what they are getting and guess at the information. What you are trying to do is get very clear impressions, not hurry through the process to astound yourself or your friend. As you are stating your impressions aloud, each time your friend confirms something you have said, take a moment to note what it felt like within your mind and your body when that piece of information came through. By the same token, when you state a piece of information aloud and your friend lets you know that it is not correct or does not seem to have any connection, take a moment to note what it felt like in your mind and your body when that manufactured image, feeling, or knowing came to you. In this way, you will teach yourself the difference between getting a good, clear, true psychic impression against instances when you are trying too hard and allowing your conscious mind to interfere.

If you allow your conscious mind a voice during psychic exercises or sessions, it will try to be helpful by providing guesswork and extraneous "facts" to please you. You want to allow only clear psychic impressions, so you must train yourself to be able to tell by the way you feel in your mind and your body when you are psychically clear. As you start training yourself, you are not seeking to play mind tricks. What you want is to be able to psychically recognize information that can be confirmed and validated by the person who owns or knows the background of the object. It's perfectly fine to be wrong as you learn the technique. As you note the difference in feeling within yourself between the information that comes with clarity and the "information" that is supplied by your conscious mind, it will help you to understand the difference in inner feeling between the two. Be relaxed, slow down, and the clear psychic energy will be easier to recognize. When this begins to happen, you will find that you quickly go deeper and become even more open to the information that the client and the object link have to convey to your psychic senses. Sometimes, you may find that when you give a client a piece of information you have received, their initial response is that they don't know that the information has anything to do with them or their question. Then, several months later they may contact you to tell you that while part of the answer you gave them in the reading didn't relate to anything they were aware of at the time, its significance was revealed as events transpired.

Don't hurry or try to force the impressions. Allow your breath and heart to slow, and change your perceptions in order to become aware of the information that is always there. Be aware that you are working to expand your senses beyond just the physical world as you connect in a focused manner with the levels of frequency and vibration that exist around all of us all of the time. Allow your whole body to listen and to receive. As you expand and leave your normal, everyday way of sensing behind, you will feel the information and it will become a part of you as you use your psychic senses in partnership with your physical mind to simply be the interpreter of the feelings and images that you get.

Experiment with the process of psychometry by asking a friend to be your experimental guinea pig in a psychometric exercise. Ask them for an object: a ring, a scarf, a favorite pen, a watch. It can be any type of small object that you can hold in your hands. Use an object that you personally do not have any particular knowledge of in terms of its history. It should be something that is in regular contact with the individual so that there is a lot of active energy associated with it. This will make the energy contact easier as you work to hone your energy reading skills with physical objects. Don't do this in the middle of a party or loud, boisterous place. Try to find somewhere quiet and peaceful if possible. Have the person you are working with hand the psychometric energy object to you and ask their permission to read for them. Then place the object in the palm of your hand, and place your other hand on top, cupping the object. Sit quietly for a few moments and do your meditative breath, relax, ground, and open your senses. After a few moments or so you may find that an image, feeling, or bit of information pops into your mind. As you receive the impressions in whatever form they come, mention each hit out loud to your friend.

Don't try to process these images at first, just state what you are receiving. Many people who are trying the art of psychometry for the first time often see or get the impression of something quite ordinary or everyday, but then are surprised when they tell their friend what they are getting, how relevant that impression is to the owner of the object they are reading. For example, you may receive the psychic impression of something mundane like a compass. When you mention this to your

continued on the next page

continued from the previous page

friend, you may be informed that they just booked tickets for a trip overseas and had not had time to tell you about it. The trick to psychometry is to stay relaxed and open, and not to be critical of the importance or relevance of any impressions you are receiving. Just relate everything you receive, whether it comes in the form of an image, an emotion, a word or sentence, a scent, or a knowing.

You may find that the impressions you are receiving seem to be skipping around, a feeling here, an image there. But as you tell your friend each impression, they may put all of the pieces of the information puzzle together for you. They know the background of the object and how all the bits of impressions you are receiving fit together. There will inevitably be impressions that you receive but that your friend does not have a feeling of connection with. File those impressions away for future reference. In fact, you may have your friend serve as a scribe during the experimental session and record all the impressions that come through. There is a very good chance that something you receive during the session will not have an immediate bearing on the matter at hand, but as events unfold and progress, its significance will be revealed.

The more you experiment with the various techniques of psychometry, the more relaxed you will become and therefore the better you will become. Your skills will evolve, and you will begin to understand just how your senses work within the constructs of psychometry, how information tends to be received within your mind, and how it feels within your body. You will become more and more comfortable with the process. You should start to experience clearer and better results as your mind becomes used to seeing the information and your body feels it. At first, you will be pleased to pick up on things correctly and you will progress in your training. The next stage is to follow and expand upon the images and feelings that you receive in your work with objects. There may be a lot more information that you can obtain as you analyze this additional information.

EXERCISE 36: USING THE YES/NO TECHNIQUE

You may find it easier to begin by asking a question of the object that can be answered with a simple yes or no. For example, as you are handling the object link, if you sense a person connected to your friend, you might want to pursue this feeling or the image you have of the other person that you are receiving so that more information is revealed about the connection and what it signifies. This involves simply asking questions in your mind concerning what you are seeing (receiving clairvoyantly) or feeling (receiving clairsentiently). Ask "Is this person a member of the family?" Do you get a feeling of yes or no? If the response feels like a no, next ask "Is this person someone from work?" If the answer still feels like no, then ask

continued on the next page

continued from the previous page

"Is this person a social friend?" When you get a positive or yes feeling as to the relationship between the person you are working with and the individual who has come up as a connection in the session, the next question to ask is, "Is there a problem between them?"

The more questions you ask, the more details will be revealed. With each question, more information will come to you and you will begin to see a bigger picture of the situation, how these people and their circumstances connect and how you can begin to suggest solutions or options. Stay relaxed and don't get into a game of guessing. Wait patiently for each answer and relay this answer to the person you are working with. As you state each question aloud and then follow it with the answer you are psychically receiving, the person you are reading for can interact, affirming information you are receiving and helping you to fill out all of the details.

Psychometry with an object link is a method that many psychics use when working with the police, especially when trying to locate a person. The psychic or medium will be given either something that belongs to the missing person or a photograph of them. The handling of the object or photograph by the psychic and the opening of their senses to the energy present around and within the object helps to create a psychic link to a missing person because of the personal energy residue that individual has left within the auric field of the object during their possession of it.

Photographs of a person or place can give you psychic impressions about someone's identity, their personality, and events that have occurred involving them. You can work to hone your skills detecting and receiving information about people or places by working with pictures given you by friends or that you see in a magazine or newspaper. One way to practice is to have a friend give you a picture of a person or place that they have knowledge of, but that you don't personally have information about. Relax and open yourself in your usual way, allowing your senses to pick up bits of identifying information as you connect with the image in the photograph. State aloud anything you are getting, any hits or nudges that come to mind, or any emotions and feelings you receive. Don't try to make up a story about the person or place, just allow impressions to float to your mind and give them voice when your psychic body sense or a feeling of knowing tells you it feels right. Have your friend confirm or deny the pieces of information to let you know when you are getting firm hits and when you are off. As your friend confirms an impression that you are stating, pay attention to your body sense and the way your mind feels when the information comes through.

Conversely, note what the information that was wrong or erroneous felt like. When you are receiving clearly, your mind will feel alert and relaxed and your body's energy field will feel clear. When you are not getting actual information, but are instead trying too hard or unintentionally filling in gaps with your imagination of your conscious mind, your mind will feel

continued on the next page

continued from the previous page

a bit stretched and cluttered and you will not be having any sensations of energy flashes within your aura.

Working with a photograph from the newspaper or a magazine can be something that you do easily by yourself. When you see the photograph, do not read the accompanying article about the individual. Instead, while gazing at the image, open your psychic senses and see what type of information comes through—why this person is being highlighted in the news article, what type of work they do, and what kind of person they are. After you have received some impressions that you feel clear about, read the article and see how accurate you were in your assessment.

Strong emotions are often stored clearly on objects due to the intense output of energy expressed during times of emotional stress or great joy. The energy imprint of dramatic events resonates powerfully in objects and spaces as well. I remember very well as a child picking up an old Asian knife at an antique show and feeling as if I had been punched in the stomach. That experience taught me to ground my energies before handling unknown things. Houses may contain psychic residue linked to an event such as a murder or suicide that occurred within its space. But intense or ongoing events that leave psychic energy behind do not always have to be ones with negative connotations. Oftentimes, people who have lived in a house for a long time and raised a family there and then passed away within the space or in another location, may stay behind for their own reasons—maybe they are unaware that they have died, or they feel a strong emotional attachment and peace when they are at the home and continue to reside in energy form within the space.

There is much legend and lore about physical locations where battles have taken place, and sometimes people who claim no psychic sensitivity at all have reported unusual activity that they did not anticipate experiencing. An example of this is the battle that took place at Antietam Creek near Sharpsburg, Maryland. This place is now called Bloody Lane and is the site of the bloodiest battle of the Civil War. The Battle of Antietam took place on September 17, 1862, and involved hours of intense and bloody fighting by the opposing soldiers on the sides of an old sunken road separating two farms. Confederate soldiers were on one side of the embankment and Union soldiers were directly across on the other side. The two groups of soldiers fired continuously at each other as each faction struggled to take possession of the site. More than 23,000 men were killed, wounded, or missing in action during this historic battle.

In her article *Ghosts of Antietam's Battlefield and the Bloody Lane*, Rickie Longfellow, writer, historian, and member of the West Licking Historical Society, Smithsonian Institute, and Daughters of the American Revolution writes:

> According to eyewitnesses, Bloody Lane is haunted. Gunfire and the smell of gunpowder have been reported when no one is on the road or even nearby. One visitor to the battlefield saw several men in Confederate uniforms walking Bloody Lane. He thought they were reenactors until they vanished. The most convincing of the reports is the one of some Baltimore schoolboys who walked Bloody Lane and heard singing out in the fields. They said it sounded like a chant or the Christmas song "Deck the Halls." They heard a chant similar to Fa-la-la-la-la sound repeatedly. The area was near the observation tower where the Irish Brigade charged the Confederates with a battle cry in Gaelic, which sounded like the Christmas carol.
>
> US Department of Transportation (*FHWA.DOT.GOV*)

Any place like this is a reservoir of strong, intense energy emanations and anyone, skilled psychically or not, will pick up on the vibrational intensity of that area. People who have developed their psychic receptors will find it very simple, if perhaps a little overwhelming, when they receive such strong, impacting energy signatures. The psychic imprints left on objects or in places can relate to any information—a location, a time, or a feeling can all be stored and contained within an object or space.

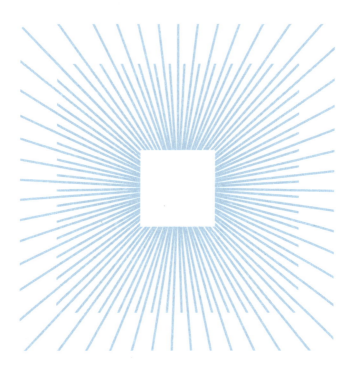

CHAPTER 9

Psychic Animal Communication and Spirit Animal Energy

Psychic messages and impressions are received and experienced through your interactions with people you encounter, as well as with spirit guides or other noncorporeal entities. You can have the same kinds of psychic connections with animals as well—those who are still living and those who have died. And in some ways, animals can be easier than humans to access and connect with psychically because of their unique ways of experiencing the world around them. Animal brains and their thinking functions work a bit differently than humans. Humans use a linear, intellectualized beta wave brain energy for their day-to-day tasks, while animals are always in a more feeling, psychically sensitized alpha brain wave state. We humans often have to train ourselves to bypass our linear way of processing information in order to move to the less linear and more abstract feeling, energy sensitive alpha brain wave activity that is the natural thinking state of animals—the state that works so well for us in psychic work and acts of creative expression.

Animals are always in this more abstract, conceptual, alpha feeling state. They are continually scanning the environment around them with their awareness in a more emotional, sensitive state, using their subtle senses to detect danger as they determine if another animal or human is friend or foe. In this state of continual and sensitive cognizance and information processing, animals remain in a psychically open condition, always acutely aware of the energy field produced by the emotions and thoughts of their human companions as well as the other animals around them. They are ready to react to any circumstance instantly without having to intellectually dissect, analyze, and interpret the situation before they act.

One can psychically communication with animals who are living as well as with animals who have passed away. First let's talk about psychic communication with living animals. When animals are living, they communicate through emotions, feelings, body language, vocal sound, and facial expressions. They also communicate through imaged thought processes, emitting a mental picture of their thought or feeling. Animals are highly sensitive to the energy emanations of other animals and of the people that they encounter, and are also psychically attuned to the environment surrounding them.

We have all experienced an animal who, when a certain human begins to approach them or enter their space, reacts immediately with hostility. The animal psychically senses that the intention of the human is not friendly to themselves or to the human companion they may be with. They sense the presence of danger or threat through their subtle senses. There are opinions that the animal's reaction is due to their acute sense of smell—they smell fear or threat due to the hormonal release of adrenaline in an approaching human. Part of the animal's reaction may very well be due to their heightened sense of smell as they analyze the situation, but it is also due to the animal's psychic awareness of the "flavor" of the energy that the human is presenting. By the same token, animals respond in a positive fashion when they sense that the intention of an approaching human is benign or friendly. How many times have you nervously watched as a child goes running wildly toward an animal, aware of the possibility that the animal may react with fear and bite or attack the child? Instead, the dog wags his tail, or the cat lies down and presents its belly to be rubbed. The animal sensed the energy intention of the child to be curious, friendly, and open and reacted accordingly.

Animals also transmit images to humans mentally of things they want us to do or help them with, but they do not use or understand language via words like their human counterparts. Animals recognize the sound of some words that are important to them in their relationship to their human friends—stay, play, out, no, lie down, eat—but they don't really know words in the literal and strung-together way that humans use them, in written sentences or vocalized thoughts. An animal's thought process is based on feeling and image. Animals are quick to react to the feelings they get from the thoughts or words of humans, and while they hear the words that we are saying, they are also receiving the mental telepathic images and emotional energy associated with those words from us as we think about what we are going to do or say next. And in the same way, animals project telepathic mental images as well as the energy of their emotional desire to us as they communicate psychically. We receive this information, and we may simply get the mental image or emotional feeling that the animal is projecting, but we also add to our interpretation of their intention or desire through a clairaudient sense of words. When we interpret what we are receiving in this way, we are receiving the animal's transmitted telepathic image, and then adding on additional interpretive information, filling it out in our human way of using human language and words within our minds to understand exactly what they are trying to tell us using image and feeling.

Would you like to find out what would make your pet happier? If your animal friend is having any pain or discomfort? Would you like to know what emotional component is behind a particular behavior? Perhaps the pet is behaving inappropriately, and its owner and companion wants to find out why the behavior is happening and get it to stop. You can connect or link psychically with an animal to get answers to these questions and more.

Being able to psychically communicate with animals is a useful skill. You may wish to find out why your animal friend is engaging in annoying behavioral issues and what those issues are linked to. You may wish to understand their health problems and the underlying cause and foundation of the illness. Maybe a pet is very sick or badly injured, and a decision has to be made to decide whether to have it euthanized or if medical treatment should be employed to bring the animal back to health. Sometimes, when working with an older animal that has been sick for a long time, we need to know what they would like us to do. Should we let them continue working on healing their illness with the help of a trusted vet while in body? Or do they actually want our help to make a gentle passing out of the compromised body their soul is currently residing within?

Wouldn't it be interesting to know the background of the pet you adopted at the shelter, or how your companion animal feels about a specific person or animal and why? What does your pet think about the quality of his or her life? What does your pet want to teach you or humanity? What has your animal set out to learn in this lifetime? Are you wondering how your beloved animal who passed away is doing and what she or he wants you to know? When we psychically communicate with an animal, whether living or no longer in body, we can get answers to all of those questions. Many times when a pet has died the owner or human companion wants to contact the pet's spirit to both receive and to give comfort.

If you have pets, you probably have wondered whether they know what you're thinking or how in the world they just reacted to something that you thought but did not say out loud or act on physically. You have no doubt experienced your cat or dog hiding or skulking around when you start planning a trip to the vet in your mind. You haven't said anything out loud about the trip. You haven't gotten the leash out, spoken the name of the clinic or vet, or even prepared the animal carrier for the visit to the veterinarian, but they know, don't they? And most of them react by trying to hide.

People who work as animal psychics—animal intuitives or animal communicators—would explain these events as the psychic intelligence of the animals. According to animal psychics, you communicate with your pets telepathically all the time, without even knowing it. Your cat hides or your dog gets ready to play because of signals or picture images you unconsciously send with your mind as you think about playing or think of the impending visit to the vet, not just because of any of your physical actions.

Does your dog run in circles or leap joyfully at the front door when you simply *think* about taking him out for a walk or going out to play? These events can certainly have a simple, logical explanation. Your dog might have seen you involuntarily glance at his favorite ball or toy. As you are mentally considering which route you want to drive this afternoon to the vet appointment, your cat does her best to turn invisible and sneak out of the room. Perhaps your cat might have gotten a whiff of the scent of the hairball medicine which she associates with the veterinarian's office. But there is more to it than that. They have psychically picked up on the thought or image as you mentally considered this action in your mind. Their sensitivity to your energy and thought waves causes them to react to the unspoken and, as yet, unacted-upon thought.

All of your life you have unconsciously directed your thoughts and emotions to the animals around you. It is through the transmission of consciously directed emotions and thought images that you can develop and use your psychic senses to understand, counsel, and connect with the animals in your life. Psychic animal communication is a combination of telepathy, claircognizance, clairsentience, and clairvoyance, and it can be very helpful in understanding your animal companion and when making decisions involving your pets. The process of making this psychic connection is the same as working with your human clients.

When you work on a psychic level with a pet you are intentionally using your mind and your emotions to communicate and talk to animals. This may be for your own personal interest in the animal or to relay information about the animal to a client or friend who lives with it. When you are communicating with an animal on behalf of a human owner or companion, you will begin initially by talking to the human companion of the animal by phone or in person. You will begin by asking questions to get information from the human pertaining to the animal's name, their age, gender, and appearance so that you can make a clear psychic contact with the animal. In addition to those basic questions, you should ask if there are other companion animals in the household and if there is a specific area of inquiry that they wish to pursue and get answers to.

You will start as you always do by grounding yourself, slowing your breathing, and moving into a gently focused, meditative alpha brain state. The animal may be physically present, or you may be looking at the animal's picture, holding its collar or a toy, or have received information from the human companion regarding the pet. This information will consist of the animal's name, its physical appearance, its likes and dislikes, its distinctive behaviors, the names and descriptions of other pets in the family, and the question or questions you are seeking to receive specific information about, such as behavioral issues.

If the animal is present physically, you will initiate the energy connection with the animal by speaking its name softly aloud and gazing toward it but not into its eyes. Sometimes animals will react to an unknown person staring into its eyes as a threat or an act of dominance, so until the animal becomes relaxed in your presence, reserve your gazing to the energy field of the animal. Observe with your clairvoyant psychic senses the animal's aura and open your mind and clairsentient senses as you begin to direct a conversation toward the animal. Tell it in general terms about the behavioral problem you'd like to address, or that you are aware of the health issue that you need their help understanding. Mention the other animals in the household that there seem to be an issue with, or talk about some of the games that you've heard the animal enjoys playing. You are creating an energy rapport with the animal and allowing it to take its time in adjusting to your presence, your smell, your energy flavor, and your emotional state. Note if you clairvoyantly see any energy flares as you mention different things, and continue moving deeper in connecting with the energy field of the animal as you work to get a sense of the animal's basic emotional state and personality.

Once you feel an ease and an energy rapport, ask a direct question of the animal, either out loud or in your mind, while you look into its eyes. Wait quietly for the response—the animal will transmit information to you via a mental image or emotional feeling that you will begin to interpret. As you receive this information, you will write this response down, draw a rough copy of a mental image you are getting, or speak aloud the type of information that is coming through. Don't judge any of the impressions you are getting with your conscious mind during this receiving. There will be time later to analyze the information using both your conscious mind and your psychic senses. Just keep yourself open to the communication and continue to record what you are getting in whatever way is most straightforward, direct, and easy for you.

When working to understand the health issues of an animal, it can be helpful to actually move your hands within the auric field of its body if the animal is present. In this way, you can sense the energy flow within its energy field and find places where the energy is blocked, is leaking energy, is devoid of energy, or has a discernible heat or chill to it. This will help you to diagnose what the problem is and how it is expressing itself in both the energy field and the physical body of the animal. After you have received health information from the animal, give that information to its human and have them follow up at the veterinary office. During the time that you are working with the animal, you can certainly apply your abilities to clearing their auric field, infusing the animal with vital energy and the like, but in addition to this psychic healing and energy balancing, the animal should also receive physical medical treatment from a qualified vet that will help to alleviate the symptoms that the physical body is experiencing.

Of course, you may also explore health issues when the animal is not present, by making a psychic distance connection with the animal once you have some information about it. Although it is nice to be able to work directly with the energy field of the animal right there in the room with you, you can do excellent energy work by extending your psychic senses to the animal wherever it may reside. This is called "distance healing." You are working with energy, and energy does not follow the same rules as physical time and space. When you use a telephone or computer to communicate and connect with someone, physical distance is immaterial. The same is true of a psychic energy connection. You can use photographs or descriptions of the animal to make contact when the animal is not present.

If the animal is not physically in the same space with you, you can begin to make the psychic energy connection by gazing at its photograph, picturing the animal's appearance in your mind, by handling the collar or toy belonging to the animal, saying its name aloud or within your mind, or all of these tactics together.

Stay relaxed and open your senses further, allowing the answers to come in an easy, flowing manner. Do not pressure yourself to receive anything, just allow it to happen. The experience is similar to mastering some physical activity like a sport: if you stay tense and judgmental of your body while you engage in the activity, you are usually awkward and graceless. When you relax and just let your body do what it knows how to do, the ease returns and you perform the movement well. It's the same with your psychic senses. If you are tense and have an impatient sense of expectation, you will stay blank. When you relax and let your senses do what you have been training them to do, you will enter the flow and receive information easily.

If you are working with health issues involving an animal, you may receive information via your clairsentient senses, including feeling a small stiffness in an area of your body, a small pain in a muscle, limb, or organ, or a sense of dimming in your vision. Any of these sensations should be slight, just an indication of the area that is affected adversely in the animal. If the sensation becomes strong or lingers, you have taken on some of the unbalanced energy of the health issue and will need to clear that energy out of your system quickly after the session ends.

You may receive a mental image that is accompanied by an emotion and you may receive the image or picture of a human who is involved with the question. You may sometimes receive a claircognizant knowing of the answer, or hear an answer inside your head or just outside of one side of your head a few inches away. The animal in this hearing clairaudient case is not literally speaking to you using human language, you are processing the information you are receiving through your human senses and the way that humans often process and interpret information is via the use of words. During the session, you may ask several questions and receive answers to each question, or you may receive answers to some but not all of the questions you have posed. When you receive partial answers to your queries or answers to some but not all questions you have asked, stay relaxed about it. Many times, as with other psychic workings, you will get more information at a later date, usually within a few days' time.

When psychically researching behavioral issues, after making the initial psychic link with the animal, state out loud what the issue is in a gentle manner. Don't be verbose. Simply say what the problem is in a few words: "Messing in the house"; "Chewing on the laundry"; "Urinating on or tearing up Tony's clothes"; "Running away during walks"; "Fighting with the other animals." Sometimes in these situations, the offending animal will be reluctant to communicate with you, fearing that it will receive a reprimand or punishment. Keep your energy light, friendly, and open just as you would with anyone else with whom you are trying to solve a problem. Repeat the animal's name again, several times, in a friendly and accepting manner. You may wish to create a visualized image in your mind of a treat or affectionate petting to send an emotional message to the animal that there is a reward at the end of all this. Once you have gained the animal's confidence, you begin to receive information from them in the ways outlined above. Relate this information to the human companion and help them to devise some solutions to the issues that are bothering the pet using the animal's input and point of view.

Bette Heller, a gifted horse trainer and caring animal communicator in the Denver area, uses clairvoyant techniques in her psychic work with animals, but also employs the technique of automatic writing in many of her sessions. She sits quietly, allowing her psychic senses to open as she creates a link with the animal she is working with, calls out their name, and thinks the questions or pictures the situation involving the animal for which she has been consulted. She tells me that she receives information in different ways depending on the situation and the disposition of the animal and the owner.

Sometimes she receives a claircognizant knowing—an immediate sense of the answer that comes in words in her mind or just outside of her head close to her ear. In some instances, the information will arrive as a clairvoyant image accompanied by other information in a knowing fashion and sometimes, when she has pen and paper at hand, as she offers the question to the pet, she simply begins writing as the animal communicates its feelings and motivations to her. She cautions that for her, as for many animal communicators, after the human companion has given her the basics to work with regarding the animal, it can be easier to get the answers a bit later when the human is not present:

> If the human won't quit chattering, or if I get the sense when I'm trying to connect with the animal that the human is feeling impatient or overly expectant, I can't get the information in as clear a way as I want. In those cases, I will give my client my initial impressions and let them know that I will be working on it and get in contact a little later when I have the whole picture.

Maybe you just want to check in with your pets. But many people seek the advice of an animal psychic for a specific reason, such as in instances when the pet is lost and its human companion wants to figure out where it is or encourage it to return home. In the case of a lost or runaway pet, it is often very useful to have a physical link such as a picture, or a collar or toy that contains the energy residue of the pet. In this type of lost object or psychometry work, you will ground and open your senses in your usual way, and then begin to receive clairvoyant mental images of the surroundings that the pet is encountering. Pay attention to clairvoyant images of distinctive landmarks such as bodies of water or unusual looking trees. The animal may be able to send you images that include street signs, but as the animal does not read, it will not process the symbols and words in signs in ways that are helpful to humans.

You will more than likely also receive emotional responses from the lost animal such as the feelings of confusion, panic, or fear. Work to create a beacon of energy and light that can help the animal sense in which direction to travel to return home. Send the animal emotional energies of comfort as you work—just like people, when animals get lost, they will panic. The calmer they become, the easier it will be for them to use their intelligence and their own psychic sense to make their way back to home base.

Unfortunately, sometimes the information you receive is that the animal is no longer in its body—it has passed away due to a predator or some tragic accident. In this case, if you are comfortable with how you are feeling and reacting in this situation, continue to create and maintain the contact with the animal, offering any reassurance or comfort to aid with the passing. Let the animal know that you will give its human companion comfort as well, and that, if they both would like, you will be available in the future to help provide communication between the animal and its human family.

Many times a deceased pet will linger in the home after its death to keep you company through your grieving process. You may spy them out of the corner of your eye as they move through the room, or hear their voice somewhere in the house. Often, animals who have passed on serve as companions for a time to the other family pets as well as the humans in the household. Until it decides to move completely on, the deceased animal enjoys the feeling of their physical world home and will maintain some interest and curiosity about the home and its former family.

A deceased pet might cause some problems with other living animals in the household. Animals are very sensitive to, and generally comfortable with, those in spirit, whether the spirit form is that of a deceased human, a spirit guide, an angelic form, an etheric entity, or their now-deceased animal friend with whom they shared the household. However, obviously the way that the living animal and the deceased animal can interact has changed. One animal still has a body, one does not. This can lead to some frustration on the part of the deceased animal as play is different and, perhaps, its human friends are unaware of its presence and are therefore not interacting with it as they did in the past when the animal was embodied. In its seeking to interact with its human and animal household friends in the same way that it did while in body, an animal can inadvertently link into the vital energy force of other pet animals in the household, sapping some of their strength and leading to illness, fatigue, or depression.

In this type of instance, psychic counseling with the deceased animal will help it to understand why the other animals and the people in the household are not interacting with it as it is used to. Oftentimes, either helping the animal move on to an energy level where it can create connections with other animal spirits, or giving the animal a task to do around the home (protecting the parameters of the home, watching out for the family children, and keeping the other animals still living in the house safe and out of mischief) can resolve problems. The pet animal that is now in spirit will be happy to perform these responsibilities until the time comes for them to move on—either further into the realm of spirit or into a new body to be reincarnated.

Speaking of reincarnation—to incarnate again into a physical vehicle for the soul assumes that there is a soul. Do animals have souls? All you have to do is look into the eyes of your dog to know he has a soul. Gaze into the intense eyes of an eagle and it is impossible to ignore the intelligence and soul residing within that body. Many times when a family pet dies, the soul of that animal will return to you in another, newer and healthier body at a later date. Give it a little time. Just like humans, after the experience of death an animal will need to process the meaning of events that occurred during the previous lifetime. But if the bond between you was deep, you can have the joy of having your companion with you again, in a different body. Of course, this is a decision that the animal must make on its own, with its own interests in mind, and you should never try to force the issue. But there are some things you can do to help your pet come back to you in another body if it is willing.

After your grieving process is over, not during, engage in active, visualized meditations involving the animal. Wait until you are truly done with your grieving and are ready to have another companion in animal form. Fondly remember his or her unique personality, a special expression they had when happy or surprised, how they would lie on your lap or stand by your side and enjoy a good scratch on a particular part of their body. When you have their image firmly in your mind's eye and you are feeling the close, special bond you shared with them, state their name aloud. Call out loud as you would call them to you when they were in their body. Use any nicknames you had for them in this calling in addition to their given name. Spend just a few minutes doing this two or three times a week. If the animal is willing and not engaged in some other type of task or work that they need to accomplish in the spirit world, they will return. It may take a month, it may take a year or two, depending on the things their soul is doing, but if they want to, they will return.

I had a cat that I did this with. In her first incarnation with me, Maxine was a decidedly eccentric seal point Siamese cat. I was the only person she seemed to like or put up with, and she was quite cantankerous, but we were very close for the nineteen years we lived together. In the last year of Max's life, she developed a tumor in her nasal passage under one eye, but until the end, she continued to eat well, continued to saunter to the different places in the house that she liked to perch, and was her prickly yet affectionate self. The last few months of that year, however, as the tumor grew and she became less comfortable, I consulted with her psychically regarding her quality of life. I wanted to know how she felt about staying on in her body: did she just want to face each day gradually losing her strength until she passed, or did she prefer to just move on out of her failing body now?

At first, she was willing to just take her daily life more slowly, sleeping more and being less agile, but during the weeks before she let me know it was time for her to pass, she became blind in the eye above the tumor, and even though she was still eating well, she was really just hair, skin, and bones. One afternoon as I sat with Maxine in my lap, grooming her and giving her little tidbit treats, she looked up at me and held my gaze intently. She then closed her eyes in a very deliberate fashion and as she laid her head down in my lap, I knew she was ready to go and it was time.

I made an appointment for the next day with her veterinarian to have her euthanized. When the morning came, Max was waiting by the cat carrier for her trip and, very differently from her previous trips to the vet, she made no protest when I put her in the carrier. Before that morning, any experiences with the cat carrier involved yowling protests and lots of claws, but not this day. When we arrived at the vet's office, I held her in my arms for a few minutes, talking to her and sending her mental images of a warm, open meadow where she could enjoy chasing birds, mice, and butterflies. The vet came in quietly and, massaging the scruff of her neck to find a vein, he injected her with a drug to put her to sleep, forever. Her right paw contracted on my hand as she squeezed me in thanks, then all of her muscles relaxed. With a long, deep sigh, Maxine left her body. I could feel her relief and knew we had done the right thing.

Of course, I was heartbroken. Max had lived a long, pampered life, probably within the only household who would have put up with her, but I was very saddened by her loss. For a few years after this, I still would notice Maxine out of the corner of my eye and would sometimes feel her brushing my leg with her back. I would hear her funny Siamese yowl coming from one of the rooms in the back of the house, and I would sometimes see her, in shadow, standing on the back of the couch where she used to enjoy watching the world go by. Whenever I would have these experiences, I would tell her that I would love to have her back again, whenever she might be willing. Then, a whole year went by with no appearances or contact from Maxine. I would think of her and sometimes even call her name to see if her spirit form would visit me, but nothing.

One night I had a very vivid dream of Maxine. In this dream, she was sitting on the counter in a kitchen. On the wall above her head was a clock numbered one through thirteen. The clock's hour hand was pointing just past the thirteen on the clock face. It didn't seem strange in the dream, but as I recalled it upon waking, I wondered at the unusual number of hours that were designated on the dream clock face. I knew it was a signal from Max that she thought it was time to come back. I started looking in the paper at the pet ads (cats only—I knew Max would never bother coming back as a dog). And I know I had to sound a little strange to the people who I called when I requested the date of birth and then politely declined seeing the kittens when the birth date was not on the thirteenth. But

I knew strongly that the number thirteen was involved and I was trying to find litters that had been born on the thirteenth day of the month. No luck, however, and after a month of this, I sat back and waited to see what would happen.

Three or four weeks later, out of the blue, the phone rang. It was my brother-in-law calling to say that his developmentally disabled son had found a litter of feral kittens under the bushes in their backyard. The mother had been a local alley cat, but she had been missing for a few days and they feared she was dead. The boy had managed to capture one of the black kittens after a good chase and told his parents that it was named Maxine, although he had never met my cat and had no knowledge of the special relationship I had had with her. My brother-in-law wondered if I wanted the kitten. I flashed back to my dream with Maxine and the kitchen clock and was struck by the fact that my brother-in-law lived in a house in between 13th and 14th Avenue.

So Maxine came back in a litter of wild kittens two months after my dream—the gestation period for a cat. She was letting me know via my dream that she was getting ready to reincarnate, and my psychic senses were giving me the information that the number thirteen would somehow be involved. When I received the new kitten, it was a boy—small, aggressive, and coal black. He was only about four weeks old and needed to be bottle fed. I named the cat Roger and his behavior made me laugh when I fed him. It was at first a bit of a standoff between us—he would back himself into the corner of the towel-lined box that we had him contained in. There he would puff himself up fiercely and spit and growl at me—shades of Max. During the feeding, I would wrap him in a small towel to keep him from drawing my blood and offer him the bottle nipple. After a moment of hesitation, he would smell the milk and make a lunge for the bottle, chewing the tip of the nipple off during the feeding in his enthusiasm. As Roger grew, he started to become less black and it turned out that he had the markings of a very dark seal point Siamese, like Maxine. His ill manners and way of sauntering around the house were very Maxine-like and I knew she had come back to me in another form.

Animal Spirit Connections

The practice of human connection and interaction with a more archetypal type of pure animal spirit is ancient and almost universal worldwide. There are many spiritual traditions that span our planet that all share the concept of spiritual connection between humans and animals. These traditions share particular techniques for recognizing and acting upon this spiritual axis between animals and people. Human and animal connection practices have been used all over the world: from South America through North America and up to Alaska; in Eurasia from Siberia to China; in the countries of the Pacific Rim, from Vietnam to Australia; in ancient Europe; and in Africa.

In the last three or four decades human and animal spiritual work and association has been termed "shamanism," but "shaman" is not necessarily the word that each individual indigenous culture uses for their practice. The word "shaman" originates from the ancient Tungu people of Siberia and Mongolia ("saman") and is used to denote men and women who, among the many spiritual functions they serve as the priesthood in their culture, are healers, interpreters of dreams and omens, weather diviners, and more. As part of their spiritual practice, they also interact with the spirit world using trance states and energy connections with spirit animals. The word "shaman" has been adopted in the Western world to describe people in any culture, such as Native American tribes or nations, who do similar work, but who may use a different title, such as medicine man. For this chapter, the word "shaman" is used in this more universal sense for practices that utilize spirit animal energies for their results.

Shamanic traditions teach that individuals can be connected to one or more different "spirit animal guides" during their lifetime. These spirit animal guides can move in and out of a person's life at different intervals depending on the person's spiritual and life journey direction and the soul tasks that the individual needs to complete along that journey. These psychic energy connections and experiences with spirit animals for shorter durations occur at times when the human needs a specific and particular type of help or protection during a period of spiritual awakening or duress. These are spirit animal guides who can help you, protect you, and lead you to personal spiritual discovery during your lifetime, but they act within your life at different times for specific reasons special to that time.

There may also be one spirit animal guide or "totem" that a person maintains connection with throughout their lifetime. The word "totem" is an Ojibwe or Chippewa word used to denote the primary spirit animal connection of a person, family, or locality. This is a spirit animal that travels with you for life, giving aid both in the physical world and the spiritual world. Though people may identify with several different spirit animal guides throughout their lifetimes, it is this one totem animal that acts as the main tutelary or guardian spirit for an individual all through their life passages. A special connection and closeness is shared throughout the individual's lifetime between this spirit animal totem and the individual. This spirit animal totem connection serves to bring insight, spiritual protection, strength, and wisdom to the human.

There are several ways in which you can determine if you have one of these spirit animal connections and discover what animal spirits are traveling with you. Perhaps you have had an ongoing personal interest in a specific animal and its characteristics from the time you were a child. Your initial interest and fascination with this animal may have begun in your childhood, but your fascination and feeling of connection has continued and probably intensified as you have grown older. Or you may suddenly develop an intense interest in a particular type of an animal. Are you drawn to figurines or paintings of a specific animal? Do you like to read articles, stories, or books about a particular animal?

This animal may begin communicating with you in your dreams, giving you information or simply being present in many of your dream stories. Do you have a recurring dream about a certain animal, or a dream from childhood that you have never been able to forget? This animal may also make itself known to you regularly in your meditations while you are in a receptive alpha-mind state.

Another way spirit animal energy can manifest its presence to you is by appearing to you as an omen or sign. When this happens, you will find that you encounter a particular animal repeatedly in a short amount of time. For example, several times in one day, a fox runs across your path, a squirrel fusses at you all day outside of your window, or a raven keeps flying over your car as you drive. Do you find that a certain kind of animal consistently appears in your life? This doesn't necessarily have to be a literal physical appearance of the animal at your doorstep. The connection can be represented in other ways, such as receiving cards and letters with the same animal pictured on the printed material over and over. You could be having repetitive dreams of a particular animal, or be watching television and see the same animal in different programs time and time again. Is there a particular animal that you see unusually frequently when you're out in the mountains, in a park, in your backyard?

These are all signs that you have a spiritual connection with that animal. If you cultivate this connection, you can receive comfort, guidance, companionship, and protection from the spirit of this animal by consciously connecting and aligning your energies with them.

This animal spirit guide offers power, protection, and wisdom via a differently nuanced perspective to the individual with whom it is connected. When the human "communicates" and links with the totem animal by paying close attention to its actions and seeking to understand what the animal is pointing out to them, this shows respect and trust. This focus and awareness on the part of the human deepens the energy connection and allows for ongoing communication. This is not the same type of relationship as that between human and pet. You do not actually pet or spend recreational time with this animal. It is a relationship of equals, and your part in the relationship is to be open to learning the spiritual lessons that the spirit animal totem is seeking to impart to you.

For some, knowing what their spirit animal totem is can be a very simple and natural process. At some level of being, they have always known that there is a connection between themselves and a particular type of animal. They have always been inexplicably drawn to the animal or had a special feeling for the animal's energy. Other people wonder how to determine what their animal totem is and how to make that connection for themselves.

If you would like to open up a connection with your spirit animal guide and discover what your animal totem is, meditate on if you have ever felt drawn to one animal or another without being able to really explain why. This animal could be furry and four-legged, but can also include birds, reptiles, fish, and insects.

What does a spirit animal guide offer you by way of guidance? They can warn you of danger or give you a nudge to pay particular attention to something. By communicating with spirit animal guides, you can take on positive attributes of strength and wisdom of those animals, have allies in the world of spirit, better understand some of the ways energy works, and receive literal counsel.

If you have access to shamanic events in your area that offer help in finding your spirit animal guide or totem, you might want to take advantage of that experience and help in finding your animal spirit. Sandra Ingermann has written several excellent books on shamanic techniques to help you in this quest as well.

CHAPTER 10

Psychic Etiquette, Hygiene, and Troubleshooting Tips

Whether you perform psychic readings just for yourself or for others, you need to receive clear answers to your questions. The process of grounding your energies and centering yourself allows you to relax, alter your state of consciousness into the receptive alpha brain wave state, and feel confident that the information that is coming through to you, regardless of what psychic techniques you employ, is clear and accurate. So before you begin any psychic work, always use the grounding and centering meditation techniques as outlined in Chapter 1. And as you ground and center yourself, extend that energy into the space where you will be working to clear and neutralize it as well. If you always open your psychic senses in a space or room that you use as your dedicated reading space, this ongoing clearing of the room will serve to remove any psychic dust bunnies from any previous sessions. And, in the future, if you perform psychic readings at psychic fairs or at a local metaphysical store, you will want to set the energy in the room or at the table you will be using to keep it clear and calm for the multitudes of different energy flavors that have been in that place. You will find that as you follow the procedures involved in grounding, before long the process will take less than thirty seconds to get into the mental and psychic energy space you need for accurate and clear psychic work.

It is important as you develop, experiment with, and hone your psychic skills that you also know how to shield yourself. I have known many psychics over the years who have become physically ill, mentally imbalanced, or delusional as to the interpretation of the information they are receiving because they did not use shielding techniques. Some have had their lives thrown into disarray because they did not follow a few simple practices that kept them from taking the issues of some of their clients into their own auric fields. I don't say that to frighten you . . . really, the ways to ground and shield are very quick and easy to perform by anyone. But they are vital to practicing your skills competently and confidently. No matter how long you have practiced as a psychic, you still need to do your basic grounding and shielding every day.

Why? You must ground yourself (by connecting your energies with those of the earth) in order to keep the information and psychic impressions you are receiving clear and accurate. If you are not grounded, you may misinterpret what you are getting. This may be due to the fact that you or the person you are reading for is in a highly emotional state and the impressions you are receiving are coming from those strong emotions, not from the actual energy currents that are working to form future events.

Sometimes, either purposefully or unintentionally, a person you are reading for can hook into your energy field and draw vital force from you. This is another reason to ground yourself before each reading. You need to have an adequate shield to prevent such an energy draw from happening. If you are reading for a client or friend who has a physical, emotional, or mental illness, you can be too open as you access their energy banks for the reading and take on aspects of the illness yourself if you are not shielded. If your client is in the midst of chaos in their life, you can be too open and allow that chaotic energy to invade your life as well.

If you are grounded, you will know how the energy is working for you and for the person for whom you are reading. You will know if you are making a clean connection and getting the psychic hits. You'll know by how you are feeling during the reading—your mind will be clear and your body will feel completely relaxed. The reading won't be work—it will be an exciting, unfolding experience. If you are grounded and shielded, you will easily be able to monitor how well the reading is going.

When a reading is very emotional or difficult due to the circumstances of the client with whom you are working, you may find that you are putting out a lot of energy amperage while you are counseling and helping them. In this instance, you can take a short break, pay attention to the connection that you have made with the earth's energy, and draw more vitality from that source. If you are grounded and working with a difficult person you can also draw up more energy from the earth to reinforce your shield. If you are not grounded, you can draw too much from your own energy reserves and end up feeling tired and confused. If this is happening, you will often find that some of your interpretations for your client are not spot-on due to your confusing your client's emotional or physical state of stress with what is actually coming together for them in the future.

Shielding can be a slightly tricky balancing act. You want to be open enough to connect with a client and assess the energy pathway they are following, yet shielded enough to not take on any of their energy. My advice is to shield enough to be able to control any energy burst or hook sent your way, but keep it as open as you can. This is called a permeable shield—energy can move back and forth through the shield as you read. If you sense at any time during the session that you are feeling tired, confused, or disoriented, you can take that short break, draw energy from the earth, and add some power to your shield. If you have to do this more than twice during a reading, I would stop working with the client for that session, send them on their way, and assess the situation a little later when you can analyze it objectively to determine the cause.

If you read for other people, you must also create, enforce, and maintain appropriate boundaries. Most individuals who counsel others do so because they are caring, giving people. They like to connect with others and help people sort out solutions to the problems being faced. As a psychic counselor, you act as a professional counselor and a healer, and this means that you do not allow your clients to become your friends. If you cross this boundary, this will cause you problems later as you strive to be objective when you counsel them. If you move into more of a social context with your client, over time you will learn too much about them, their problems, and their relationships. This social information that you have about them can often cause you to doubt some of the psychic information that you are getting—you won't be sure sometimes if it is actually psychic information or just advice that you would like to give them on a personal level. You will also find yourself editing the way that you give them psychic answers to their questions because you won't want to cause them distress or you feel like you want to make the situation they are facing look rosier. Not that you ever want to be so blunt with anyone who you are counseling as to be hurtful or disrespectful, of course, but when working with people you have a personal relationship with, that relationship can inhibit your communication style with them.

In addition, many times clients do not understand that you actually don't have all the answers (you are not omnipotent and the truth is that people must also be proactive in discovering and implementing solutions to problems in their life) and you cannot and should not be available to them day and night. If you charge for your services, allowing the client to become a friend can also muddy those waters, and they can begin to think that because you have developed your gifts, you owe them, as a friend, access, without compensation, to those gifts. You might also find that a few of your clients regard you as a pythoness on a pedestal and begin to insist that you be the one who gives them all the answers to their life's problems. Oh, and yes, eventually you'll fall off that pedestal and reveal your feet of clay, but when it happens it will be unnecessarily messy and no fun for anyone.

I'm not saying that you cannot or should not read for your friends or family. You want to share your gifts and you should. However, you cannot allow anyone to take advantage of your time and skills—you will develop a very unhealthy relationship with a demanding friend if you allow yourself to be used. You will become resentful of them and they will be resentful that you used to be so compliant and now you're drawing a line. Friends can be very helpful with feedback as you try out new techniques and skills by giving you timely feedback about the accuracy of your work. Just don't allow a one-way relationship to form where you feel you must perform in order to maintain the friendship.

One last pitfall when you read for a friend or family member: you already have opinions about, knowledge of, and a history with people close to you. When you have this information, it is actually harder to read for a person objectively, and not just use your tarot cards or other tools to give you an excuse to tell the person your exact opinion of a situation they are facing. You cannot inject your opinion—you must stay neutral, give them the information they are seeking, and let them make their own decisions.

There are also people who will want to prove you wrong. They deliberately or unconsciously close their energy off to you during a reading, making it very difficult to connect with them to sense the information. You don't have to prove anything to anyone, so don't take the bait. Just let them know that you are not having the usual easy time of obtaining information for them, thank them, and send them on their grumpy way.

If you use psychometry as part of your psychic repertoire, do not place any pieces of jewelry that you will be reading on your person—no watches on your wrists, rings on your fingers, or pendants around your neck. This will create a bit too much of a psychic link and can lead to some of the energy associated with that object moving into your auric field on a semipermanent basis, until you take steps to clear the energy from yourself.

Remember as you work with disembodied spirits when doing medium work, or when you use a talking board, that just because a person is dead or a spirit is in an energy form, it does not mean that they have all the answers. They can give you information about the things they knew while in body, or messages about spiritual matters, but they don't know everything. Before you act on any message or information that you receive from a spirit, confirm the veracity of the message by physical world means.

If you do any work with clients that involves energy balancing or healing, during which you will also be physically touching your client as part of the session, check with your state and local statutes as to what type of licensing must be obtained to legally touch a client. You may need a massage license, a psychotherapy license, a minister's certificate, or the like to be able to use physical touch in your work. It would also be a good idea to obtain some basic liability coverage in case you run into any trouble with a client. You can usually attach an insurance rider to your home or office insurance policy for little or no money in the event of a lawsuit.

Sometimes, when people first begin psychically counseling other people, because they are so enthusiastic about the help they can provide others, they don't pay attention to their own psychic, mental, emotional, or physical health. Just like overdoing anything, this can lead to fatigue and burnout. This fatigue and burnout can result in physical illness, which rest and a break will easily take care of, but of more concern is the mental and emotional toll. It's easy to tell when you are physically tired, but when the fatigue involves one's mental and emotional state it is often not as straightforward to see. When you are emotionally or mentally burned out, you can fall prey to delusions about your psychic work and the real state of your reasoning processes. If you read for other people, keep your schedule as regular and reasonable as you can—no more than four days a week. You will need the other three days to take care of your mundane affairs and to live your own life. You need other creative things and interests to occupy yourself with beyond psychic work as well. By keeping your life in balance you will keep your psychic work fun, rewarding, and clear.

Be respectful of the boundaries and privacy of others—it is not ethical to snoop psychically into someone else's life. When someone asks you to read for them, they are giving you permission to connect psychically with them for a brief time. No matter how curious you may be, or how much you believe you can help someone, reserve your psychic work with them for those times when they have requested that help.

If you find that, on occasion, you are wrong about a prediction you have made, don't despair or take it too deeply to heart. You're human, not perfect. Being wrong is a great lesson that can teach you about keeping your psychic energy clear, and about being aware of the way your body feels when you are in sync with the energy flow and when you are not. Being wrong can show you things about how you may sometimes pressure yourself during a reading to impress or perform for someone—ego is never a good lens for psychic work.

As you work with others, work with humility and compassion. Pay close attention to how you are giving your client information. Do not be dire and frightening, even if the psychic information you are getting is troublesome. Present what you are getting honestly, but always couple difficult information with suggestions for what your client can do to make the outcome a more positive one. And for those fun readings where everything looks fantastic, be sure to remind your client not to rest on their laurels—inaction can lead to less positive results if they just sit back and don't keep attending to their goals as they have been doing. You are working with them to give them objective, unbiased information. Do not interject your personal opinions in the matter.

Always engage in discretion and confidentiality in terms of the problems and information that anyone you are reading for has shared with you. Your client rightfully expects that what they are telling you will be held in confidence. Do not engage in gossip or tell others about anything that a client has shared with you.

There may be times in your psychic work that you are to unable to make the psychic connection. You sit down to do the session and seem to be drawing a blank. You may be experiencing a time when you need to take in and absorb all that you have been learning. It's time to take a break and let the conscious and subconscious minds process all that you have been involved in. Don't worry—you will be psychically open again. Just relax and enjoy a little rest.

Here are some troubleshooting tips for keeping your space and yourself clear of unbalanced energy.

CHARGED ETHERIC ENERGY CLEANSING WATER

You will need:

- ✧ Spring or undistilled bottled water
- ✧ A gallon-sized jug
- ✧ ½ cup lemon juice, apple cider vinegar, or ammonia
- ✧ 4 pinches of salt
- ✧ Herbs such as rue, hyssop, sage, or basil (optional)

Place spring water or undistilled bottled water into a gallon jug. Add the lemon juice, apple cider vinegar, or ammonia and four pinches of salt to the water. Let this mixture sit out in the sunlight from sunrise to sunset. You may elect to add herbs such as rue, hyssop, sage, or basil to the water as well. Pour some of this charged water into an open container that you keep by your bedside to absorb excess or unclear energy (don't drink it), or add it to a purification bath for yourself when cleansing the energy of your aura.

PURIFICATION BATH

Draw water into your bathtub. Add the charged water to the bath. Begin by completely immersing yourself from head to toe. Lie comfortably in the bath and as you soak in the hot water, imagine all stress, imbalance, and negativity being drawn out from both your physical body and your aura into the water. Stay focused mentally on the purpose of your bath and recite a prayer or invocation of purification and protection. When you are ready, unstop the tub but remain in the bath and imagine all negativity and imbalance draining out of the tub, away from you along with the bath water.

BREAKING A PSYCHIC ENERGY CONNECTION

If, during a reading, you feel that your client or some thing is sending you negativity or making a connection that you don't want with your aura, first draw your dominant arm (the side you write with) down across the front of your body to break the contact. Next cross your arms over your solar plexus (stomach), and then cross your ankles. Redo your shielding and you should be good to go. If this happens again during the reading, stop the reading and break off contact with that individual.

GROUNDING YOUR ENERGIES AFTER PSYCHIC WORK

After any psychic work, be sure that you have a snack or eat a light meal. Seal your aura by using a "closing sign"—a procedure of using a physical movement that signals your aura to close down—stamp your foot, clap your hands, place your hands on the ground to release any excess energy, or move your arm in a downward motion across your body in front of your diaphragm.

STONES TO HELP YOU STAY GROUNDED AND CLEAR

✧ Clearing: clear quartz, rose quartz, bloodstone, amber

✧ Grounding: hematite, onyx, jet

✧ Strengthening: tiger's-eye, black tourmaline (especially of aura)

Using your psychic abilities is an amazing and rewarding gift that can bring help, comfort, understanding, and self-confidence. May it be a blessing to you and to others.

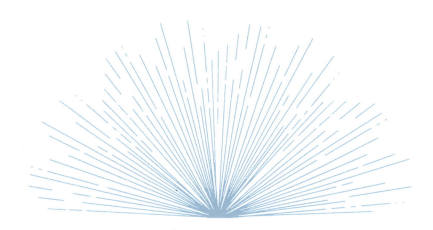

SUGGESTED READING

In my decades of psychic work and research, I have read some wonderful books. If there is an area of psychic study that you are particularly drawn to, you may want to consult some of the books I have listed below. Unfortunately, many of these books are no longer in print, but most are available as used books on Amazon, or you may want to ask your local librarian for help. Titles that are no longer in print have been marked with an asterisk.

Adler, Vera Stanley. *The Fifth Dimension.* York Beach, ME: Red Wheel/Weiser, 2000.*

Andrews, Ted. *How to Do Psychic Readings Through Touch.* Woodbury, MN: Llewellyn Publications, 2005.

Butler, W. E. *How to Develop Psychometry.* York Beach, ME: Red Wheel/Weiser, 1979.*

Capra, Fritjof. *The Tao of Physics: An Exploration of the Parallels between Modern Physics and Eastern Mysticism.* Boston, MA: Shambhala Publications, 2000.

Cunningham, Scott. *Sacred Sleep: Dreams & the Divine.* Freedom, CA: Crossing Press, 1992.*

Eason, Cassandra. *The Psychic Power of Animals: How to Communicate with Your Pet.* New York, NY: Piatkus Books, 2005.*

Farmer, Steven D. *Animal Spirit Guides: An Easy-to-Use Handbook for Identifying and Understanding Your Power Animals and Animal Spirit Helpers.* Carlsbad, CA: Hay House, 2006.

Garfield, Patricia, PhD. *Creative Dreaming.* New York, NY: Ballantine Books, 1985.*

LaBerge, Stephen. *Lucid Dreaming: A Concise Guide to Awakening in Your Dreams and in Your Life*. Boulder, CO: Sounds True, 2004.*

Lynne, Carole. *Consult Your Inner Psychic: How to Use Intuitive Guidance to Make Your Life Work Better*. San Francisco, CA: Red Wheel/Weiser, 2011.

Macy, Mark. *Spirit Faces: Truth About the Afterlife*. San Francisco, CA: Red Wheel/Weiser, 2006.

Michele, Desirée. *Enhance Your Psychic Abilities Through Automatic Writing*. Sedona, AZ: Infinity Books, 2006.*

Mickaharis, Draja. *Spiritual Cleansing: A Handbook of Psychic Protection*. Boston, MA: Red Wheel/Weiser, 2003.

Miller-Russo, Linda, and Peter Miller-Russo. *Dreaming with the Archangels: A Spiritual Guide to Dream Journeying*. Boston, MA: Red Wheel/Weiser, 2002.*

Muhl, Anita M. *Automatic Writing*. Whitefish, MT: Kessinger Publishing, 2003.*

Paxson, Diana L. *Trance-Portation: Learning to Navigate the Inner World*. San Francisco, CA: Red Wheel/Weiser, 2008.

Penczak, Christopher. *Spirit Allies: Meet Your Team from the Other Side*. Boston, MA: Red Wheel/Weiser, 2002.

Sargent, Denny. *Your Guardian Angel and You: Tune in to the Signs and Signals to Hear What Your Guardian Angel Is Telling You*. San Francisco, CA: Red Wheel/Weiser, 2004.

Talbot, Michael. *Your Past Lives*. New York, NY: Fawcett, 1989.*

Taylor, Joules and Ken Joules. *Clairvoyance: How to Develop Your Psychic Powers*. York Beach, ME: Red Wheel/Weiser, 2001.*

Ullman, Montague, MD., Stanley Krippner, PhD, with Alan Vaughan. *Dream Telepathy*. Charlottesville, VA: Hampton Roads, 2002.

Weiss, Brian. *Many Lives, Many Masters: The True Story of a Prominent Psychiatrist, His Young Patient, and the Past-Life Therapy That Changed Both Their Lives.* New York, NY: Fireside, 1988.

White, Ruth. *Working with Your Guides and Angels.* York Beach, ME: Red Wheel/Weiser, 1997.

RESOURCE

Although Charles resides in the Denver, Colorado, area, he has a wonderful website and is available to give you help as you discover your psychic talents.

Charles Cox was ordained as a Spiritualist Minister in 1991 at the age of twenty-nine. Today, using his humor and insight, Charles teaches others to communicate with the so-called "dead," helping them to build a closer relationship with the ever-present Spirit World. He says,

> I believe that developing your psychic abilities has real tangible benefits; not the least of which is finding a new sense of confidence in your own life. Once you begin to discover that Spirit is always there in your life wanting to guide you toward your greatest happiness, it is easier to navigate life challenges.

To find out more about Charles, go to *www.charlescox.info*.

INDEX

Michael, 80

mistakes in predictions, 197–198

P

past lives, 102, 113–116, 134-139
mother-daughter case, 123–124
recall, mirror technique, 128–132
sacred contracts, 124–125

physical body
past lives recall, 130–131
soul and, 117

physical space
past lives recall, 128–130
sacred space creation, 31–32

Powers, 76–77

prayer, angelic energy and, 83–84

precognitive dreams, 95–98

Principalities, 76–77

psychic boundaries, 197

psychography. *See* automatic writing

psychometry, 46, 151
best practices, 196
clairaudience and, 157
claircognizance and, 157
colors, 152
energy link, 158
experiments with friends, 161–162
handlers of objects, 157
items best suited, 152

lost pets, 179–180
magnetic energy and, 156
photographs, 165–166
physical locations, 167–168
police work, 164
questioner's subconscious, 156
yes/no technique, 163–164

purification bath, 200

R

Raphael, 81

Ratziel, 79–80

reincarnation. *See also* past lives
animals, 183–185
definition, 113–114
karma and, 118–122, 125–127
soul and physical body, 117
teachings and, 118

relationships, soul mates, 125

REM (rapid eye movement) sleep, 94–95

S

sacred contracts, past lives and, 124–125

sacred space, creating, 31–32

Sandalphon, 81

scrying mirror, 20, 132–133

self-care, 197, 200–201

Seraphim, 76–77

shamanism, 186

shielding energy, 192–194

sleep stages, dreams and, 94